BRITONS THROUGH NEGRO SPECTACLES

About the Author

A. B. C. Merriman-Labor was a barrister, writer and munitions worker born in Freetown, Sierra Leone, in 1877. His published works include *A Series of Lectures on the Negro Race* and *The Story of the African Slave in a Nutshell*. He also edited two editions of the *Handbook of Sierra Leone*. He arrived in the UK in 1904 to study law. In 1907, he organized a centenary commemoration of the abolition of the slave trade in Westminster Abbey. He later embarked on an 'entertainment-lecture' tour called *Life and Scenes in Britain*, travelling across thousands of miles of West, South West and Central Africa, which he expanded on to create *Britons Through Negro Spectacles*.

BRITONS THROUGH NEGRO SPECTACLES

A. B. C. Merriman-Labor

With a new introduction by
Bernardine Evaristo

PENGUIN BOOKS

PENGUIN BOOKS

UK | USA | Canada | Ireland | Australia
India | New Zealand | South Africa

Penguin Books is part of the Penguin Random House group of companies
whose addresses can be found at global.penguinrandomhouse.com.

First published by The Imperial and Foreign Company 1909
First published with a new introduction by Penguin Books 2022

001

Additional Contextual Notes compiled by Danell Jones and S. I. Martin

Set in 11.6/15 pt Fournier MT Std
Typeset by Jouve (UK), Milton Keynes
Printed and bound in Great Britain by Clays Ltd, Elcograf S.p.A.

The authorized representative in the EEA is Penguin Random House Ireland,
Morrison Chambers, 32 Nassau Street, Dublin D02 YH68

A CIP catalogue record for this book is available from the British Library

ISBN: 978-0-241-55974-1

www.greenpenguin.co.uk

Contents

Contents

Contents

Publisher's Note

In this book are some expressions and depictions of prejudices that were commonplace at the time it was written. We are printing the book as it was originally published because to make changes would be the same as pretending these prejudices never existed. At the same time, we have chosen to redact the word 'n——', which appears frequently throughout the text, in recognition of the particular harm this word enacts and in the belief that contemporary readers should not have to endure that harm in order to access important literature.

Introduction

It's such a pleasure to introduce readers to this buried treasure of
a book, *Britons Through Negro Spectacles* (1909), written by the
Sierra Leonean writer Augustus Boyle Chamberlayne Merriman-
Labor. It's a travelogue and social commentary in which he
subverts the colonial ethnographic gaze on Africa and repositions
it on to the occupants, culture and customs of the colonial heart-
land, London in particular – an incredibly audacious conceit at a
time when the British Empire was at its peak.

The book's numerous chapters have headings such as 'Britons,
Blacks and Bargains', 'The Invisible Spirit of the Britons', 'White
Women and Black Men', 'Frocks, Frills and Flounces' and 'Matters
Moral, Immoral and Unmoral'. The author adopts the persona of
a character who is acting as a tour guide to an imaginary person
he refers to as 'Africanus', explaining the city and culture to him
as they perambulate across it.

While his speech is obviously aimed at Africans who haven't
been to Britain, he's actually establishing his superiority over the
imperial nation. Authoritative, knowledgeable, witty, mischievous, he comments on the high and low of street life in great detail,
from the finely dressed to the beggars in rags who sleep in the
gutters – and everyone in between.

Humour pervades the book, yet in its preface Merriman-Labor

states that 'one of my aims in writing is not so much to be humorous, as to reveal truths spoken in jest'. He is indeed a satirist, who explains his approach thus: 'Considering my racial connection, and the flippant character of literature which, at the present time, finds ready circulation among the general public, I am of the opinion that the world will be better prepared to hear me if I come in the guise of a jester.'

In such a guise he tells us,

> . . . most Negroes agree with Darwin that the Blacks come from the ape. As regards the parent of the Whites, the common Negroes differ . . . They say that the original ancestor of white people is the grunting creature – the filthy pig . . . The common Negroes in a mirth-provoking manner argue that, because the skin of the pig as seen at the butcher's resembles that of a white man, therefore the white man is the child of the pig.

Pretty daring stuff, right?

Through his observations, we also discern differences between Africa and Europe. When he describes the scale and scope of London's geography and buildings, with a population of six million, he unwittingly reveals the comparative smallness of African cities. When he says that an underground train buries a person 'when alive, three hundred feet below ground', we know that tube trains do not yet exist on the African continent. The necessity to describe snow as 'rain which comes in the form of white powder' makes clear its absence in most of Africa.

A churchgoing Christian, Merriman-Labor disapproves of the busy public activity in the capital on the Sabbath and notices, tellingly, that sermons 'did not threaten the hearers with "the everlasting fire and pain" as missionaries are accustomed to do in West Africa'.

So who was Merriman-Labor, one of Britain's earliest black writers? Not much was known about the author until the first biography about his life, *An African in Imperial London: The Indomitable Life of A. B. C. Merriman-Labor*, by Danell Jones, was published as recently as 2018. Well researched and comprehensive, it's my primary source for what I've learned about the author. I urge people to read it to find out more about this exceptional man.

Born in 1877 in Freetown, the capital of Sierra Leone, Merriman-Labor, a brilliant student, left school at sixteen owing to lack of funds and worked briefly as a schoolteacher in the Gambia. With literary aspirations, his first work of fiction, a story called 'Building Castles in the Air', was published in the *Gambia Intelligencer* in 1895, before he reached the age of eighteen. This was followed by other publications including *A Series of Lectures on the Negro Race* and *The Story of the African Slave in a Nutshell*. He also edited two editions of the *Handbook of Sierra Leone*. For his pamphlet *The Last Military Expedition in Sierra Leone* he adopted the pseudonym 'An Africanised Englishman' – to hide the fact that he was a black man.

Eventually, Merriman-Labor joined the civil service in Freetown, saving up for six years in order to visit Britain. Jones tells us, 'He saw the written word as his weapon against the injustices of colonialism, and London as his literary home.' We also discover that he'd read in the *Sierra Leone Weekly News* that, once in the city, 'colour would be no barrier to recognition'.

When he arrived there in 1904, it goes without saying that he discovered the opposite to be true. Still, he found employment as a clerk and a teacher in Stockwell, and used his savings to study law at Lincoln's Inn. At the same time he set up the African General Agency, with the aim of facilitating better business relations between Africa and Europe. However, this was a commercial enterprise, which contravened the rules of engagement at Lincoln's Inn, and he was forced to close the agency. As if studying law wasn't enough, in 1907 he organized a centenary commemoration of the abolition of the slave trade in Westminster Abbey, no less. Clearly enterprising and energetic, before he was called to the bar in 1909 he also embarked on an 'entertainment-lecture' tour to Africa called *Life and Scenes in Britain*, travelling thousands of miles through West, SouthWest and Central Africa, which he expanded on to create *Britons Through Negro Spectacles*.

This book, unsurprisingly, was trashed by the critics upon publication. The *Law Journal* damned it as 'valueless' and the *Daily Express* decried its 'low jests'. Deliciously feisty, wild and high-spirited, flipping a finger at the colonial overlords, it's astonishing to think that it was written over a hundred years ago, but unfortunately the author was a century ahead of his time. Far from being welcomed into artistic circles, he was ultimately cast out and ended his life in penury. Renouncing his English name, he changed it to Ohlohr Maigi. During the First World War he worked as an inspector in the vast complex of the Royal Arsenal munitions factory in Woolwich, where I grew up, as it happens. Interestingly, my mother's grandfather and other forebears worked in that factory. Perhaps they knew him, or knew of him. He certainly would have been noticed as a black man at that time.

By the end of the war, Merriman-Labor had contracted terminal tuberculosis, dying in the Lambeth Workhouse Infirmary in 1919 at the age of forty-two. I like to think that if the author had arrived in Britain as a young man towards the end of the twentieth century, instead of at the beginning of it, there would have been so many more options available to him and most definitely more interest and support for his writing. For someone of his intelligence, activist spirit and GSOH, he might have been a comedian commenting on social injustice, or a leading human-rights barrister. Perhaps he'd make films and documentaries about aspects of African history or Sierra Leonean society; or he might become a publisher, academic or Member of Parliament. Instead, he was a daring challenger of a society that thought he had no right to answer back, no right to hold a mirror up to their own attitudes; a society that was not 'better prepared' to accept his good-natured jesting.

Some of his books and pamphlets are in the British Library for further reading, and I hope the reintroduction of this book as part of the Black Britain: Writing Back series, coupled with the biography by Jones, will see him resurrected from obscurity and re-evaluated as a significant writer and figure in our literary history.

Bernardine Evaristo
August 2021

Preface

The outline of this book has been presented in the form of entertainment-lectures entitled 'Life and Scenes in Britain', which I delivered to hundreds of Europeans and thousands of Africans, during my recent tour of fifteen thousand miles through West, South-west and Central Africa. The favourable reception given to the lectures has encouraged me to enlarge on, and otherwise to amend them, with a view to this publication.

As regards the style of writing used in the following pages, I may say that, for the sake of clearness and simplicity, I have adopted a somewhat diffused phraseology with a bias towards repetition, emphasis, tautology and conversationalism.

It has been said that mine is a humorous style. In fact, the leading West African periodical, whilst commenting on the lectures which are the groundwork of this publication, referred to me as the Negro Mark Twain. I shall indeed be sorry to be regarded solely as a humourist, for one of my aims in writing is not so much to be humorous, as to reveal such truths as may be best spoken in jests. Considering my racial connection, and the flippant character of literature which, at the present time, finds ready circulation among the general public, I am of opinion that the world will be better prepared to hear me if I come in the guise of a jester.

I prefer Bible references to others. I do not thereby admit that, at my age and at this age, I am prepared to accept many of the orthodox interpretations given to passages in the holy book. I prefer scriptural quotations, because they are a thousand times more worldwide in their application than national ones.

A book which is here and there scriptural, and is in part humorous, will, no doubt, help to confirm the great doctrine of Edmund Burke that the sublime has always a ridiculous counterpart. You may therefore expect to find in *Britons Through Negro Spectacles* much sense and nonsense, facts and fiction – the old, the new and the 'novel' concerning Britons and Blacks, the whole treatise running, in the words of Nicolas Boileau, the French poet and critic, 'From grave to gay, from lively to severe.'

A. B. C. MERRIMAN-LABOR
London, August 1909

Chapter One
Taste and Foretaste

When as a little boy I became persistently naughty by bellowing continuously at the top of my voice, to the great discomfort of the household and the annoyance of my Uncle Jim who was then reading for the ministry, my mother would quiet me by shouting, 'The white man is coming, the white man will come and take you away.' If I did not wish to go to school, or to be forced into bed when fowls went to their roost, she would still raise the same shout about 'the white man coming'.

In course of time, I did not care a rap about the kidnapping white somebody whose advent she daily predicted, for this sluggish individual always by the way coming – coming – coming – like the final Judgment, never once arrived.

At this stage of my indifference and consequent troublesomeness to a greater degree, Uncle Jim, forgetting that he was a candidate for the Church, assisted Mother to deceive me again into good behaviour. When she cried that the white man was coming, Jim hid himself behind the door, and there, with a voice which Mother kept repeating was the white man's, growled continuously in a coarse gruff manner that shook all naughtiness out of me.

After a while, having got accustomed to this second trick, I did

3

not think anything of a big white man in hiding who seemed much afraid to meet a little black boy face to face. His power, I fancied, merely consisted in the strength of his deep bass voice over my shrill piping one. However, this opinion was quickly changed when, one morning, a person with a horrible white face did appear. His features were enough to cause myself and my stubborn naughtiness to take a final flight into the region of oblivion.

He had such a long and pointed nose, two prominent cheek-bones and a protruding chin which resembled a third cheek-bone. This three-cheek somebody owned, besides, a pair of dancing eyes which appeared at the bottom of deep hollow sockets. To all these, he added two ears, in size, just those of a deer. On the bargain, because his lips were thin, and his mouth extremely wide, his teeth were as frightful as those of some horrid monster. The dreadful sight of this fierce-looking white-face demon, completely convulsed a bad little black sinner into a good little saint.

I gave little or no bellowing trouble thence forward, until I grew big enough to learn not to dread the mischievous Uncle Jim when he wore, over his face, the devil-mask painted in the colour of a white man's skin.

And by that time, years having hardened my body, whenever I shrieked or bellowed, Mother either plastered warm adhesive slaps on my face, or, what was worse still, bamboozled my bare behind with the cumbrous walking-stick of her age-bent grandmother.

Whilst we think on the story of the bogey white man, thousands of children, here in Africa, are being frightened by a cry similar

4

to 'the white man is coming'. Strange to say, not only children, for, a whole village of raw natives in some far interior country would, at this very moment, vanish into the bush at the approach of a single white person. Besides, not only raw natives, for, even in the minds of civilized Negroes, there lives a feeling that there is something not natural about a white man. The white individual is some sort of superhumanity: so many Blacks imagine.

Thus, somehow, in other words, the notion seems to exist in the mental somewhere of a good many black people, civilized and uncivilized, that the white man is a premature return from the spirit world. Such Negroes also believe that they themselves will become white when they die. These funny notions are born of the idea, which some entertain, that ghosts and the devil are white. In this connection, it is to be remembered that pictures of the devil as illustrated in books of white missionaries and intended for black people, have usually been painted in the white man's colour. This fact affirms, and perhaps assists to create, the idea now current in the minds of millions of black people that white men belong to the supernatural creation of angels, ghosts and devils.

Having regard to the circumstances just related, and to other circumstances which I need not now mention, it may be said that the Whites have always been a mystery to the Blacks, just as the Blacks have ever been to the Whites. This, a mystery to that: the one, a puzzle to the other.

'Where do the Whites come from?' is a question which commenced to trouble the brains of black thinkers from the time white thinkers began to ask, 'Where do the Blacks come from?' The great English thinker, Charles Darwin, answering these two

5

questions, said that Whites and Blacks came from certain species of the baboon-ape. But long before he said that, some Negro thinker had given nearly the same answer to this dual query.

In consequence, to-day, most Negroes agree with Darwin that the Blacks come from the ape. As regards the parent of the Whites, the common Negroes differ. They declare that the forefather of the Whites cannot be as manlike as the ape. They say that the original ancestor of white people is the grunting creature – the filthy pig.[1] Their reason, a simple one, is thought out in a more simple way. The common Negroes in a mirth-provoking manner argue that, because the skin of the pig as seen at the butcher's resembles that of a white man, therefore the white man is a child of the pig. Hence some common Negroes often say of any objectionable white man, 'That dirty, filthy, white pig.' Laugh a bit, before you listen more.

If I am to answer the two questions which have from time immemorial puzzled black and white thinkers, including the arch-thinker Darwin, I will say, 'From many points of view, Whites do not know Blacks, and Blacks do not know Whites.' We, as members of the great human family, ought to know something about the Whites, and, as British subjects, first about the Britons. These people can best be seen and known in their capital City of London, as there Britons from every corner in Britain may be found. So, in thought, spend a day with me in London.

Chapter Two
Babel in Babylon

'But is London itself a place worth knowing?' you enquire.

It will take me a year and more to tell you all about the first Metropolis in the British Empire. It is a huge county – I may even say, country – for it can easily swallow, according to the latest calculation, seventy places the size of Freetown in Sierra Leone, the largest city in Colonial West Africa.

London is not only greater than Freetown in respect of area, but also as regards the number and arrangement of its buildings. In round figures, the buildings number three-quarters of a million. Huge, tremendous, sky-scraping concerns – these buildings are. I have seen one by Saint James's Park, fourteen storeys high, something probably approaching the Tower of Babel. Two thousand rooms in a public building is nothing extraordinary. Usually such a structure, when not divided into apartments, would possess a sitting and standing capacity of twenty or thirty thousand. That is to say, a London public building can easily accommodate the entire population, and half again, of Accra the capital of the Gold Coast Colony.

You will notice when in London that the residential houses in most streets are all joined together. It may then occur to you that, as one house resembles the other, a stranger who does not remember the number of his residence, stands a chance of finding himself in the bedroom of the next-door neighbour. Should he so find himself, he would, I daresay, be ejected with kisses – no! not with kisses, but with kicks and blows.

It is absurd of you to say that a London householder will fear to eject a Negro with kicks and blows, because a Negro happens, as it is, to be the champion boxer of the world at the present time, and because, as you think, Negroes being so numerous in London, they will help a comrade to retaliate with kicks and blows. Allow me to correct you by stating that Negroes in London do not much exceed one hundred, and that if even all are champion experts in the manly art of boxing, it will take them no time to see how foolish it is to attempt to use physical force against the Whites, for, number for number, Negroes are simply a nonentity in the great Metropolis. To every one Negro there, there are over sixty thousand Whites.

In other words, the population of Greater London totals considerably over six million souls. Think what this means. A thousand in one thousand places, is one million. Six thousand in one thousand places, and more than that, represent the number of London's inhabitants. Greater London is so extensive, its highways and by-ways so countless, its inhabitants so multitudinous, that although five hundred persons die in the Metropolis every day, one may go for weeks together without meeting a single funeral. If the people of London were filed one behind the other, one foot apart, they would extend three thousand miles, the distance between Great Britain and her oldest West African Colony, Sierra Leone. If you stand at a busy time of the day, at any busy spot, such as that before the Marble Arch by Hyde Park, in one single hour, there will pass you, to and fro, no less than twenty thousand foot passengers. On the day of any great race, such as the Football Final Cup Tie at the Crystal Palace, be prepared to see a myriad of people which no man can number, people as abundant 'as the stars of the heaven, and as the sand which is upon the sea-shore'.

Chapter Three
Capital Capitally Capital

The great population of the Metropolis of London, at least, any section of it, being at any given point therein, can be moved in no time to any other point, by means of the endless streams of vehicles which deluge the extensive Metropolis. I speak advisedly of 'streams of vehicles'. I have been told that twenty thousand trains enter London every day. There are over twenty railway termini in London alone, belonging to more than twenty different systems of railway, owning, as they do, throughout the United Kingdom a mileage capable of twice encircling this mighty universe. Apart from trains on railways, other vehicles in London are so numerous that four thousand have been counted in one hour in front of the Marble Arch.

There, as at any other centre, you may have the best opportunity of noticing the volume of London's vehicular traffic, as well as the different assortment of vehicles comprised in such volume.

You may notice, first, the cab for two, intended for a fellow and his precious partner. It is said to be, to some, one of the best London places for love-making on the 'q-t'. If so, cabby, the driver whose seat is at once towards the top and back of the cab, is not supposed to know. Anyhow, the cab for two is certainly more secluded than the cab for four.

Cabs and the fee-fond cabby are unknown, as you are well aware, Africanus, in this, the western part of our continent. In fact, vehicles common in West Africa, are often uncommon in London. As another instance, I may mention that sedan chairs, much used by the gentry here, are not used in London, except by the sick and the dying.

The gentry and the great in London, the elect and the select – 'gods that have come down to us in the likeness of men', use or misuse the private motor-car.

The imitation sect of the elect and select – a set of men 'who would appear to us in the likeness of gods', use or abuse the public motor-car.

Let me here say that motors have been known to cover one hundred and twenty miles an hour. Motor-cars are therefore fast, and so are some motorists. I mean the elopement-loving and the kidnapping motorists. These, I understand, long for the time when the flying aeroplane will mount them away from the wrath of a pursuing husband, or the reach of a shooting father.

Speaking of fast motors calls to mind the slow horse-drawn omnibus. But the somewhat maligned horse-drawn omnibus is not as bad as the motor-omnibus, for the latter smells so(le). And yet, the motor-omnibus is not as bad as the electric tram, for one tram with its eighty passengers, crowds together more tramps and non-tramps than two motor-omnibuses together. Still, the tram is not as bad as the overhead train, for the smoke of the latter helps to make London quite foggy in winter. Notwithstanding, the overhead is not as bad as the underground train, for the latter buries a person when alive, three hundred feet below ground.

I am here reminded that there is, as well, an Underground London – a place lower than the street pavement.

There is such a London; for, below the pavement-ground, in the gutter, are the poverty-stricken loiterers who find themselves lower than the rest of mankind.

Below the gutter men is a class of persons whom the loiterers regard as slaves, and who certainly have not the enviable or unenviable liberty of the do-no-work.

I allude to the humble men-servants who, if their daily complaint is true, have more brass buttons on the outside of the pockets attached to their long-tail evening suits than bronze pennies in the inside of all their pockets. I am inclined to think that men who wear evening suits in the morning and at noon will always complain.

I allude also to the 'maids of all work' whose white pinafores help to lessen the blackness on their faces and hands. I have never been told that these black-white women object to the colour on their faces.

These people, men and maids, have to attend to the requirements of domestic service, often at the basements of houses usually underground, below the depth of the gutter men.

Below the servants in the basements are the sewage men who, considering their job, are certainly lower than the domestic servants.

Below the sewage level, but certainly not below the social

standing of the sewage men, are the men of the water pipe, gas pipe, gas light, electric light and electric telegraph.

Far below these, there live and move, by night and day, hosts of other persons. I say so because, lower than some underground railways, are the subterranean foot-tunnels, such as the Rother-hithe or Blackwall, each several miles long, through which an endless procession march daily. It seems wonderful.

Still more wonderful to think that, whilst a concourse of people may be inside a tunnel four hundred feet or so below ground, it is possible for the River Thames with a crowd of vessels to be above the subterranean passage, bridges with thousands of foot passengers to be above the vessels, tramways with numberless vehicles to be above the bridges, railways with throngs of passengers to be above the tramways, whilst companies of telephone workers are suspended on wires far above the railways. And yet, above tunnels and river and ships and railways and trams and telephones and crowds of persons, walkers and workers, other crowds would be footing the upper span of the Suspension or Tower Bridge three hundred feet above high-water mark, whenever the lower span is bisected and raised in order to make a passage for ships.

London is therefore Overhead and Underfoot, Overground and Underground, Terrestial and Celestial.

Chapter Four
The Visible Spirit of the Britons

Of course it would be impossible for you to see these different parts of London during the few hours at our disposal. We shall therefore confine our walk to Central London where people meet on business during the day, and to West London where they meet for pleasure at night. If you will walk about the first City in the British Empire arm in arm with Merriman-Labor, you are sure to see Britons in *merriment* and at *labour*, by night and by day, in West and Central London.

The most prominent position in Central London, a position whence we shall start westwards, is the area opposite the Mansion House, the official residence of the Lord Mayor, the Chief Magistrate of the City.

If we visit the Lord Mayor, history will, in a way, repeat itself. You would remember that an ancient Chief Magistrate, Solomon, was visited by a number of persons who, according to several commentators, were Africans. I mean the Queen of Sheba and retinue. They presented Solomon, on the occasion of their visit, with 'much gold and precious stones'. Should we visit London's Chief Magistrate, we need not present him with gold and precious stones. None whatever of such precious presents for him; for, I daresay, the Lord Mayor – if not himself, then, his relatives – have subtracted, extracted, or abstracted (whichever it may be) for themselves enough gold and diamonds from West and South Africa already.

In any case, his official residence is in the very heart and centre of British wealth and finance. Nearly all the leading commercial houses, some of which can boast, each, of a turnover of a hundred thousand pounds in one day, besides all the most important financial institutions in the United Kingdom, are in the immediate neighbourhood of the Mansion House.

Conspicuous among these institutions is the famous Bank of England. I was once allowed to visit its gold-weighing room. That visit revealed hundreds of thousands of loose sovereigns on the counters. I merely saw the sovereigns 'through a glass darkly'. I did not touch them, not because I would not, but because I could not. I had been warned by the writing on the wall within merely to 'look but touch not'. I heard then that, at any time, there would be within the vaults of the Bank about fifty million pounds of solid cash. I was also told that the Old Lady does an annual business which runs into billions of pounds sterling.

I now think of all I saw and heard, and I am convinced that the Bank of England, situated as it is, in front of the Mansion House, and surrounded as they are by the great financial institutions before mentioned, renders our proposed starting point the richest spot on earth.

Hence the expression, 'All roads lead to the Bank.' But the roads leading to the Bank of England are so zig-zag, for London was formed hundreds of years ago when there was no surveyor, and when everyone made out for himself short cuts and narrow paths through commons and waste land. Zig-zag or not, Africanus, let us hurry to the Bank. That is the place I long for. Away we go! From West Africa we are flying thither with the wings of thought. It is now nine o'clock of a morning. The Bank of England is in sight.

Wonderful! Wonderful!! What mighty jostling crowds, huge waves upon huge waves of living humanity! See how 'multitudes upon multitudes' rush hither and thither, helter-skelter-like, with so much motion and commotion, verging and converging in all directions, in and out and through themselves, some on foot, others on horse, others besides on wheel. What moves so mightily these innumerable caravans of men, women and children? What energizes these moving pyramids of human ants?

I answer. The keen necessity to live, the consequent struggle for existence, the means for such existence, gold – the means, gold – the god of this world, *gold – 'the visible spirit of the Britons'*.

Chapter Five
'The Man in the Street'

As we stand here, outside the Bank of England, the waves of these rivers of human heads continue to surge towards us, to surge from us, waves succeeding waves on all sides, as far as the eyes can reach. And further than the eyes can reach. Distance away, out of sight, those receding waves, as swellings to other waves, will continue to surge and roar throughout the furthest extensions of these rivers of mortal beings.

And these human rivers in London never cease to flow. Day in, day out, at full tide or low tide, they course and re-course the many basins and creeks which pervade London's expansive plains. At night when it would be ebb tide in the basin opposite the Bank of England or that fronting the Marble Arch, it might be full tide in the newspaper creek of Fleet Street, high tide in the flower and fruit haven of Covent Garden, spring tide in the milk estuaries of railway stations, flow tide in the fish bay at Billingsgate and flood tide in the meat harbour of Smithfield.

Whatever the state of the tide may be, the rivers of street humanity here are never dry. They are always full – full with what you will please allow me to term conglomerations upon conglomerations of droplets of living humanity. Let us stand on this site, before the Bank of England, and note some units of humanity who find themselves in London's rivers of multitudes.

We cannot help noticing, first, the stalwart policeman, fine fellow, six feet high, fifty inches round the chest. As he lifts a single hand and a staff, the mighty river of vehicular traffic ceases to flow. His only staff, like the band-master's baton, can ease at once the sounds and roars of a concourse in motion.

Powerful Bobby, the dread of breakers of the law! He knows how to catch a thief, except when he himself is the thief. I mean that Bobby is so fond of stealing the valuable time of the maid-cook, if he happens to meet her when on duty in some quiet suburban lane.

Just cast a glance a bit behind Bobby. There, you see, goes the clock-like postman who every hour, from noon till night, raps the door 'rat-tat' when he brings an ordinary letter, and 'rat-tat, rat-tat' when the delivery consists of a parcel or registered packet. Armies, of which he is a unit, muster hourly to disperse within the United Kingdom some ten million postal packets every day. The postman is always welcome when a fellow is on the lookout for a love letter, and most unwelcome when it is time for a troublesome solicitor to demand an unpaid bill.

Like an arrow, the newspaper boy on his bicycle has darted in and out of the mighty traffic of horses and vehicles and vanished. The paper boy, the postman and the policeman are the three most vigilant characters in Britain.

Another vigilant character is the fireman. He is on land what Jack Tar, the sailor coming hence, is on sea – a fighter of fire.

Jack Tar, as you see, is coming arm in arm with his friend Tommy Atkins the soldier. The two are the pride of the British people. Tommy and Jack can make a match for any British foe. But one man has made and can still make a match for them. That matchless man is the African 'fuzzy-wuzzy'[2], the fighting Sudanese. He is matchless; for, according to Rudyard Kipling, he

> . . . *is the only thing that doesn't give a damn*
> *For a regiment o' British Infantree!*

Kipling shouts in further praise of him, 'He broke a British square.'

As we speak of the Sudanese, we see a Japanese man. The man of little stature comes on this side to learn from the Western. Clever fellow! He is already teaching his teacher. People at one time thought that he was not a man, that he did not possess what every other man owned. But since he was able to convert whole armies of men into helpless women, he became acknowledged everywhere as a man indeed.[3]

That little girl is not Chinese although she wears her hair in a pig-tail plait. Such a plait indicates that 'she, sweet sixteen, has never been kissed.' So, boys! give the British lass a chance. Take off your hat, and let her pass.

The boy who has taken off his hat, rather, the barehead boy who wears a long blue coat and yellow stockings, is a student of Christ Hospital or the Blue Coat School as it is generally called. He comes from Horsham where the headquarters of the school now are, no doubt, to spend like yourself a day in the City and West End.

The other lad in uniform is the intelligent but playful messenger boy. His company will charge the sender a shilling an hour for the time he takes to hang behind the costermonger's cart whilst whistling tunes suggestive of bananas and oranges.

The third lad in sight, ill-clad and miserable-looking, is the wandering street boy. His younger brothers are seldom met now-a-days on the road. Thanks to the efforts of the Guildford Street Foundling Hospital which picks up the youngest the very day of his birth, names him according to the street in which he is found, and brings him up a respectable member of society. Thanks also to Dr Barnardo's Homes which rescue the second brother as soon as he begins to walk, and finds for him, when grown up, a decent livelihood, often, in one of the Colonies, the West African Colonies not excepted.

The cart following that on which the messenger boy hangs himself is the stretcher of the ambulance men. They are carrying some poor fellow who must have been crushed in the traffic. Perhaps the poor man is dying. If so, he wants a doctor of body, or a priest – the doctor of soul.

Ah! a priest is coming. He is the servant of the Great Physician who has prescribed that he is not 'to put on two coats'. I shall dismiss the priest without any certificate of character, for, in my opinion, he is a right down disobedient servant. Quite wilfully, he openly disobeys the anti-two-coat rule. Such is the truth; for he wears a long frock coat which equals two ordinary coats of most other men. Besides, this disobedient servant quadruples his two-in-one outer garment by adding an undercoat or vest with a double front. In further addition, under the undercoat, as it is well-known, he wears an inner coat or undervest. No wonder people have remarked that some priests 'clothe themselves in purple and fine linen, and fare sumptuously every day'.

Chapter Six
The Other Man in the Street

The priest – the brother of mercy, has gone by. He is followed by a lady, once a sister *for* mercy, now a sister *of* mercy, the Salvation Army lassie. Notice her hat, Africanus! Though young, she seems quite old under that old-fashion poke bonnet-hat popular many years ago.

Another woman, that coming yonder, also wears a poke bonnet. She must be old. I can now see her face. She is old. She, tottering, is bowed with the weight of eighty winters. Give her a helping hand, young man! You may be old some day.

The other tottering woman is trembling under the weight of poverty. Herself and the baby in her arms – a baby which by a very recent law she is not to carry, both of them being so ill-fed and ill-clad, look such objects of pity. She dares not beg, as it is not lawful to beg in this country. She therefore pretends to be selling boxes of matches, one or more of which the compassionate may take in exchange for a penny or threepenny piece. She pins on herself a somewhat large card with the words, 'Kind friend, have pity. I am the mother of eighteen, all starving.' Eighteen! and yet in this already over-crowded country. Her case is indeed one for public pity. But it seems to me that domestic pity is the primary thing.

The third individual tottering along is neither like the woman of eighty winters – old, nor, like the mother with rags and tatters – penniless. He has a little money snatched from some simpleton by means of gambling, by betting hourly on horses, or by card playing. If not, his little money is swooped from some much simpler simpleton by the confidence trick. Or, this little money, he long-arms by picking the pockets of the simplest simpleton – the man who goes through a crowd without protecting his pockets.

With his ill-gotten wealth, this tottering middle-age individual reckons his advancing years by the days he spends in the 'jolly fine company' of men, and – what is more surprising to us modern West Africans – women as well, brothers and sisters of the meeting place round the corner. There, they worship and commune with Bacchus, the thirst-quenching god of the Grecians.

Being the most devoted of the many undevout worshippers, this individual across the road, is usually the last to leave the church of Bacchus. Whenever he leaves, as he does now, a gait which indicates a top-heavy head, staggers his disagreeable fish-smelling person against peaceable citizens who may be on the roadway.

The police ought to protect good people from the unwelcome advances of this disturber of the peace. The police, unfortunately, will not employ his staff on his top-heavy head, or punch his red nose. That officer's baton cannot be used on his occiput, because so long as the bibber staggers but does not fall, Bobby dares not touch him – this confirmed, if not confounded, pillar to post and post to pillar totterer.

The other male totterer is a very poor man, the poorest of the poor. His home is the fruitless park during the day. His residence is the hard and cruel street bench during the night. The street bench, when the warm sun no longer lightens it, is so hard and cold that this homeless wanderer cannot manage to lie outstretched on it. But he *must* not lie outstretched on it. If he does, the policeman will, instead, outstretch him on a bench-like bed of the prison. He ought to spend the night in the workhouse. But he does not like the house of work, as, as he says, the food there cannot strengthen the man who will work. He is always pleading that he prefers the workshop to the workhouse. No doubt he does not like work. Someone guessed that he was never taught to work, that he never worked all his life. Perhaps the truth is that he cannot find work.

Whatever may be the truth, he joins the large army of unemployed. As such, he may be seen any day in the street parade of the battalion of Foodless Marchers. Otherwise, he is to be found at an open-air class of very extreme Socialists who teach that Britain will certainly overbalance herself and tumble into the ditch of perdition, unless the burden of wealth is balanced equally on the shoulders of the rich as well as on those of the poor.

Now that this poor man in sight is not in a Socialist class or on parade, like his sister whom we have seen, he pretends to be a seller of something. Take that boot-lace from him and give him a penny! Although you do not want a boot-lace now, Africanus, it may come in handy some day. His face – how bloodless!

Poor man! He may as well throw away his filthy broken boots, for they cannot cover his toes, nor prevent his feet-soles touching the ground. Although he wears a winter overcoat this hot summer day, under which he adds a great coat, then a lounge coat, besides a shirt, not to mention an undervest, his whole accoutrements and perquisites being supplemented by a pair of baggy trousers fit for any fat Goliath of Gath, the skin of his waist can be plainly seen. Notwithstanding, there is something about him which calls for fair comment. In one respect he resembles an ancient royal personage. His finger-nails appear every inch like those of Nebuchadnezzar, when the latter's 'nails were like birds' claws'. In imitation of that king, he prefers the dew to water, and attends to his toilet without the forgotten luxury of a piece of soap. By looking through the beehive holes in his clothes, I can plainly see that his trade as a gutter merchant has not been a paying one.

The other gutter occupier is the sandwichman. He is enclosed in a board of advertisements in front of him, another at back of him and a third over head of him. These boards, coffin-like, prevent him making his bed on the bare dust of the cold grave. He thus becomes a thing of a man buried when alive.

Chapter Seven
Another Man in the Street

The third gutter occupier is the noise-making organ grinder. Busy people often drive him with a penny so that he can betake himself and his music to oblivion, if he likes. Not infrequently, he is not driven with a penny. When not so expelled, he is hastened headlong away by the bark of a savage dog, or by a bucket of dirty water showered after him by some quixotic old woman. The same beastly treatment is often accorded his sister, the shrill-voice street singer. These noise-making people should learn that though music hath charms, *charms* is only one step removed from *harms*.

The milkman is another noise-maker. As early as five o'clock of a morning when tired London is asleep, he would be heard with his shout of 'milk eh! milk eh!' The milkman should know that although we are fond of chalk and water, especially when they are mixed with a little of something from the cow, we do not like drinking chalk when we are fast asleep. If the chalk is administered while we are awake, it may perhaps change us Blacks into Whites.

I trust the Anti-Noise Abatement Prevention Association, wherever that august society may be, will look after the noisy milkman and the likes of him. Their solicitor should advise that the association commence prompt action at law against, each and all, the milkman with his 'milk eh! milk eh!', the screeching Punch and Judy show-man with his two funny-looking dolls, the organ grinder with his Ta-ra-ra-bom-de-ah, and his frail sister who skrieks —

> *There is a better land,*
> *Far, far away.*

Why do not the whole lot of these noisy mortals betake themselves and their noisome noises 'far, far away'?

It is to be sincerely hoped that the Chancellor of the Exchequer will levy a tax of a shilling on each pastry or cake of the muffin boy who invites us to taste his sour edible by ringing a devilish sort of handbell across the road. The costermonger too should be taxed according to the quantity of sound he belches out.

As regards the Salvation Army band and that of the Church Lad Brigade, Parliament ought to pass an Act making it unlawful for the Brigade to beat their bass drums wherever a man may be found, and declaring that the Salvationists should only blast their trombone for the enjoyment of the four-feet residents of the Zoological Gardens. Moreover, Parliament should see that the Christmas waits who squeak and screech and scream like a school of fighting, scratching cats on the housetop, be chained and iron-jacketed between the middle and end of December each year.

I have nothing good to say about the crack-voice coalman, or about the dirty, dust-making dustman. I have something worse to say concerning the black chimney-sweep and the black-hand boot-black. The n———minstrel is the worst sinner of the lot, if

worse than the music hall actor who blackens and n—— his face.
I wish that all these fiends and their friends, rascals who are made
black as a result of their profession, or who make themselves black
for the purpose of their profession shall, some day, find it very
black and warm with Beelzebub. Have mercy! What have I just
said? I must be charitable. Let me say that, instead of themselves,
I hope that the coal on their bodies will help to keep hot and burning the fire in the abode of Lucifer.[4]

The only street noise maker who ought to be tolerated is the
flower-girl. She brings some cheer and gladness in this world of
sin and sorrow. I think, therefore, we may well afford to hear
more of her usual shout which runs, 'Who will buy my roses?
Nice roses, three a penny.' Here is a flower-girl trying to sell roses
to that well-dressed gentleman, and that flashily dressed lady.

Who are they? I really cannot tell. They appear just the same
as any other of the thousands of well-dressed people we now see.
Perhaps this flower-buying beau with an immaculate frock coat
and a twelve-inch chimney-pot hat is a City clerk. Perhaps he is
a clergyman in plain clothes. For aught we know he may be a lord,
or a prince for that matter.

The flower-buying belle, attired as she is, in a rich dress of
velvet, is as much a mystery to me as the gentleman. She may be
a shop-girl, a countess, or a society lady.

Of course society people – members of the upper tens, when
they walk the streets like ordinary mortals, bring themselves, to
my mind, within the class of 'the man in the street'. A member of
the upper class who owns in the West End a 'four thousand pound'
motor-car and a 'five hundred pound' dog is, when on the

pavement, much the same as any average member of the numerically great middle class, and is perhaps not much better-looking than a decent member of the struggling lower class. It is true that the level streets level most men. The street makes each and every one '*the man in the street*'.

Chapter Eight
The Mixed Multitude

From the men and women you have seen and are now seeing while standing before the Bank of England, you will readily understand that the Metropolis contains all sorts and conditions of men – good, bad and indifferent.

I quite believe that London, or West Europe for that matter, is not the only place with bad people. West Africa has its bad men as well. But the bad man in the country of the Blacks, is a different being from the bad man in the country of the Whites. The former achieves his badness by using more body than brain, often under cover of night, and the latter by using more brain than body, usually in broad daylight. Out in West Africa, the scoundrel who would help himself to a few of your coppers, or the worthless old overcoat bequeathed to you by your mother-in-law's deceased god-uncle, approaches your house at dead of night when you are fast asleep, takes hours to undo your door or window, or to dig a man-hole through your wall. Whilst, in West Europe, the artful dodger who would live like a lord at the expense of your diamond pin or purse of notes, has only to give you a friendly hand-shake or a gentle tap on the shoulder while saying, 'Kind friend, beware, motor-car coming.'

I am speaking from experience. Do not think I have played the trick of the artful dodger. I have not been the villain. On the contrary, I have been twice the victim.

On one occasion I was journeying between Carlisle and Edinburgh. I found myself in a compartment with some strange men, well-dressed fellows, apparently highly cultured, without doubt excellent conversationalists, and very friendly disposed. They seemed to have met in the train by chance. After we had been in company for nearly two hours, one of them expressed a desire to have a five-pound bank-note changed. He was going to a small village half the way, where it would be difficult to have the note cashed. The other men declared they had only three pounds among themselves. I was appealed to for the difference on the security of this note. 'You can hold the note,' they said to me, 'for you look every inch a gentleman. Change it at Edinburgh. Meet us one o'clock at Waverley Station. We shall be pleased to receive our due then.' The proposal was all in my favour, I imagined. I examined the note, found it, as far as I could judge, a genuine one. I parted with two precious pounds of British money. On reaching Edinburgh, I tried to cash the paper-coin at a bank. But strange to say, the bank authorities nearly put me under arrest for uttering a bogus bank-note. I left Edinburgh wiser but poorer.

The other experience I gained in Paris. An apparently wealthy Englishman whom I met by chance, asked me to breakfast with him the next morning at a restaurant on the Boulevard Saint Germain. When there, he ordered a most sumptuous fare and drank the best wine. Breakfast being over, he asked leave to go to a place of convenience at the back of the restaurant, as the coffee, he said, was rather strong. That was the last I saw of him. About an hour afterwards, the proprietor presented me a bill for the breakfast of two. The fare, he assured me, had been ordered in my name. I tried to explain, but the more I tried, the more inquisitive passers-by continued to crowd around us. I then had a feeling that it would be amusing to them to see a white man and a black man quarrelling over some black figures on a white sheet of paper. To avoid a scene, I quietly paid the bill, after wishing the absconded scoundrel all the bad luck he deserved.

The scoundrel inspired me with confidence in himself, as did the set of men I met on the railway. In the same way, innocent simpletons are being victimized every day on this side. Every day here, one sees inside the public vehicles an inscription telling good people to 'beware of pickpockets – men and women'. I always like to read this warning, because it hints to me that people here, like those elsewhere, consist of the good as well as the bad. In fact, there are, as I have remarked, all sorts and conditions of men in Britain.

Here are congregated Whites and Blacks and Yellows[5], the workless and the workshy, the unemployed and the unemploy-able, rich and poor, high and low, the gay and the great and the gentry, paupers and peers and princes.

There are more Scotchmen in London than in Edinburgh, more Irishmen than in Dublin, more Roman Catholics than in Rome, a thousand times more Jews than in all Jerusalem, and thousands upon thousands of Gentiles who are not Britons.

Chapter Nine
Egypt's Ten Plagues

We have stood too long here, before the Bank of England, watching the crowds as they pass us, up and down. Let us begin our walk about London. You will enjoy it, the day being so lovely and sunny. You seem surprised to hear that this is a sunny day. Well! It is sunny enough for this part of the world.

The climate here is so different from ours. The British weather to people from the sunny clime, is a veritable 'ten plague of Egypt' concern. I mean what I say, and I shall prove what I say, even step by step. First plague: Water turned into (blood or) flood. Second: 'Lice' is (L, i.e., 'ell or) fire and i-c-e. Third: I am getting rather mixed up in the head. Which are the other plagues? I have forgotten their order. But I remember full well that they consist of (murrain or) more rain, flies and frogs, boils and blains and chilblains, thunder and hailstones, darkness by fog, death of the Briton's first born by winter influenza. In addition, death to the African who does not pay sufficient attention to the pinching of his stomach or the shivering of his back.

Do not be frightened needlessly, Africanus. This is summer time, a period which corresponds in a rather distant way to our dry season. The winter, according to a similar method of comparison, can be remotely likened to our rainy season. Remotely likened – because with us, as you are aware, it rains only at stated months in the year, whilst here, it rains, rather drizzles, all the year round, and more frequently so in the winter. The winter also makes more noticeable the great difference between the British and African climates, in that the night here, then, is several hours longer than the day. The longest night is in December when daylight may be only seven hours, for the sun, at the worst time, rises after eight o'clock and sets by three.

But we seldom see the sun then as it is often very foggy. The fog, at times, is so thick and black, that if you stretch your hand it will be impossible for you to see it. Then the day becomes practically night. We must light all the lamps even at noon. The nervous dare not venture out, unless guides with thick blazon lights known as devil fires, lead them for a penny each across places where two streets meet.

It may be so cold then, that our drinking water often becomes ice. During the cold, rain comes in blocks of ice or hailstones, one of which is sometimes as large as an egg of the hen. All the rivers and lakes and even parts of the sea would then become as hard as rock, so much so that thousands of people could, at the same time, skate, jump and dance on what two days before was a mighty river on which vessels were moving.

I ought to have told you that it sometimes snows. Snow is rain which comes in the form of white powder, and which in a few hours buries the ground, in certain places, two feet deep. It is a beautiful sight to see a heavy fall of snow. Just fancy, all the roads, roofs of buildings, trees and everything else, under the broad canopy of heaven, being covered over in all directions with a thick blanket or sea of white.

Then, in winter, notwithstanding two undervests each with a double front, to which are added a pachydermata overcoat, a son of the sunny clime would feel, from top to toe, like a log of ice.

As I have said, Africanus, you need not dread the weather, because it is now midsummer. We have, at this time of the year, more sun than anything else, for it is daylight as early as two o'clock in the morning and nearly as late as ten o'clock at night. I am sure it will delight you to-day to see the lovely gloam at evening time, about which lyric poets have written so charmingly. Now all nature is gay. We are glad to welcome the singing birds back again, to see the beautiful flowers on the lovely terraces and squares, and to see the parks covered with thick foliages of green. The ladies everywhere are looking exceedingly attractive in their beautiful dresses. Even the gentlemen now try to appear bright, if not foppish, in their multi-coloured suits. This is the time to be merry. The theatres and music halls are being crowded to overflow. All Britain is astir. Railway and seaside excursions and holiday-making are the rage. Let us go out and enjoy the delights of London in so glorious a summer day.

Chapter Ten
One and One Not Two

'Keep moving!' Do you hear the stern order of the policeman? I had told you that we have stood too long here, before the Bank of England. If we do not move, we may be arrested as suspects. Put your arm in mine. Let's get along.

Arm in arm we have crossed to the other side of the pavement and are on the move.

The street in front of us as we look westwards, is Cheapside, the great retail centre of the City; and the spire at Cheapside, is that of the famous church of Saint Mary-le-Bow, the bells of which can convert into a Cockney, that is, a Londoner pure and simple, any child born within its sound. If Bow Church can convert into Cockneys strangers who come within its sound, you and I become Londoners now that we, here at Cheapside, hear one of its famous bells strike the hour of eleven. We not only hear the bells, but we also see a beau and a belle near Bow Bell.

This road is *the* Cheapside. You say it is a cheap side. Do not be misled by mere names.

35

What is in a name? That which we call a rose
By any other name will smell as sweet.

Shakespeare, in whose *Romeo and Juliet* these words are, seems to have understood that a good many names in London are as misleading as, if not more misleading than, English words ending in o-u-g-h. I think you remember the foolish tricks of that rascal syllable. I cannot forgive that part-word for having once disgraced me when a mere brat of a school boy. At a spelling lesson, teacher said c-o-u-g-h is pronounced as 'koff'. So, when I reached t-h-o-u-g-h, I pronounced it 'thoff'. Although this seemed the more reasonable pronunciation, my fellow pupils regarded me that day as their best laughing stock. Fortunately for me, teacher came to the rescue by explaining that English pronunciation is very eccentric, but he did not say whether English people are. He stated further that o-u-g-h has seven sounds, which he taught thus:

> *'Tis not an easy task to show*
> *How o-u-g-h sounds; since* though,
> *An Irish* lough *and English* slough
> *And* cough *and* hiccough *are allowed to*
> *Differ as much as* tough *and* through:
> *There seems no reason why they do.*

I now repeat after teacher. ''Tis not an easy task to show how' names of places and things in and near London mislead the stranger. I give instances. The stranger is misled to think that there is a sea at the suburb of Chelsea or that of Battersea. He is surprised to find no shore or ditch at Shoreditch or Houndsditch. Nothing like a gate can be met at Ludgate, Bishopsgate, or Highgate. No similarity to a bar appears at Temple Bar or Holborn Bar. No shadow of a field exists at Snowfields or Moorfields, no cross at Charing Cross or King's Cross, and no hill worth the name at Ludgate Hill or Cornhill.

Elm Park is not a park but a street. I do not remember having seen a single elm throughout the district of Nine Elms, nor an only oak in all Sevenoaks. I saw but one dial at Seven Dials, and no sister at Seven Sisters Road. The City Temple is not a Jewish temple in the City. The Middle Temple is not a temple but an Inn of Court like Lincoln's Inn which, in turn, is not a drinking inn like a public house inn. Still, Furnival Inn is not a drinking inn, but the ground on which the Prudential Assurance Company building now stands. And so, Cheapside is not a centre for cheap goods.

'Then, Cheapside belies its name,' you ask. Refer to history for an answer. I have often found in history, recent or remote, the best answers to many existing difficulties. If people will only consult history when they cannot reconcile certain ways of African life, if you will only consult history when you do not understand why certain things in Britain are so peculiar, in many cases the right explanation will be forthcoming. If you refer to history, you will find that Cheapside has not belied its name, but that it has outlived the meaning of its name.

History tells us that in Roman times when this great London was only a small Londinium – to give it its ancient name – barely half a mile square, Cheapside was the central meeting place in the City, its forum or market being the chief attraction. Hence the Saxons who came after the Romans, called it 'chepe', that is, 'the market'; and the streets nearby now bear the respective names of Poultry, Milk Street, Bread Street and Wood Street, just to mention a few. Being a market centre, its value kept increasing time after time; and to-day a square foot of ground there, as at any other leading centre in London, would cost as much as a hundred pounds.

Cheapside then becomes Dearside. In justice to the Cheapside tradesmen, I am to add that his goods are often dear from the standpoint of price, but not from that of quality. His prices, in the words of Longfellow, are 'not what they seem'.

Chapter Eleven
Britons, Blacks and Bargains

Here is a shop at Cheapside dealing in general clothing and outfit. The pair of boots in the show case is marked 4s. 11¾d. Quite an attractive price! It allures us inside. A nice young lady appears. After making a pleasing bow, she says, 'Good morning, sirs. What is your pleasure?'

'A pair of boots, miss,' I answer.

'Ah!' she says, 'the latest fashion in boots is one made at our own works. It has just been patented, sir, and so you can get it nowhere else. It is called "The Perfection". Such nice pointed toe, broad welt and an elegant appearance. I am sure it will fit you ever so well.'

'What is the price, miss?'

'It is only 49s. 11d.,' she replies, 'and it is by far the best boot in the market for that price. It will last twenty times as long as any other. The price up to yesterday was 70s., but a reduction has been made to suit patrons of our annual auction-sale now proceeding.'

'Young lady, I want nothing so dear.'

'Will a 39s. 11½d. pair be too much, sir?'

'Have you nothing still less, miss?'

Listen how she replies to my question.

'How much would *you* like to pay, sir?'

'What about the 4s. 11¾d. pair in the show case?' is my question against her own.

'Oh! that pair is of no use,' she answers. 'The uppers are made of very inferior American oilcloth, and the soles are cheap German stuff. It will last no time. Perhaps you will try the "Durable" at 15s. 11¾d. mite. It is British made by British labour.'

The 'Durable' is brought.

'But pardon me, miss, you charge too much for the "Durable". I know I am a foreigner, but please ask the price you generally charge Englishmen.'

'We have no two prices here. We charge Englishmen and foreigners alike.'

These words she utters in a tone which deceives Africanus into believing that she has a partial liking for foreigners. As I know too well the tone and the trick, I reply:

'I have heard that tale before and often, young lady. You can be sure that I am not so green although I look so black. I am not a Briton, but I am proud to say that I am a Britisher. Unless you accept 10s. for the "Durable", I must leave.'

At this point of our wrangling, as I appear to be looking for the door, she quickly prevents my seeming departure by saying:

'Just here, please, sir. Take the pair for 12s. 11¾d. mite and half mite. Quite a bargain for that price.'

'Well, young lady, I really cannot pay that amount. I think the pair not worth more than 10s. We have wasted enough time over this affair.'

'Allow me, sir, half a second to say that you are having the "Durable" at absolutely the cheapest rock-bottom price. The charge for a similar pair five weeks since was 50s. The recent fire at Northampton which compelled the manufacturers to supply boots below cost price of labour and material, as there were no warehouses in which to stock them, gave us the opportunity of buying them cheap and to sell them four weeks ago at 40s. The thought of the early termination of the lease of this establishment made us reduce the price three weeks past to 30s. The subsequent illness of the proprietor who is now at the point of death, suggested a further reduction last week to 25s.; and the present auction-sale has placed it within reach of the public for 15s. 11d. mite. On your account, I now ask 12s. 11d. Is that too much still?'

As she stops at this point to take breath, luck gives me an opportunity to say:

'Good-bye, miss. I will allow you no further chance, not the tenth of a second, not even "half a mo", to say one word more.'

Suiting the action to the word, I commence, whilst thus replying, to walk with Africanus towards the door.

'Take it, oh! take it, for 11s. 6d.,' she, quicker than ever, feverishly interrupted. 'I do not mind losing a few shillings just to make a customer of you.'

I approve of the amount as reduced. A cheap price and a sweet voice allure us back to the feet of beauty and of bargain. To make sure I have made a bargain, I once more inspect the boots as they lie on the counter in front of the fair and sweet-tongued seller. She orders another lady, a junior assistant evidently, to bring a second pair, one that has not been unwrapped.

'You can try the boots, sir,' says the junior assistant who has just brought in a new pair.

Whilst saying so, she, sweet creature, gives a pleasing smile, hands us each a chair heavily cushioned and covered over with bright velvet. She brings a stool similarly cushioned and covered. I rest my feet on the stool. The pleasing thing of a beauty helps me to undo my old pair and to put on the new one. Look at her fingers! With what grace and sweetness those elegant fingers play on the laces of my boots as they are being tied. So much fuss is being made of me.

Africanus becomes jealous. He thinks some fuss ought to be made of him too. He does not see why those lily-white hands should not touch his ebony-black feet. 'Then buy a pair, my man,' I say to him. He buys one. He is shod with the same fuss, the same lovely play of the fingers, the same velvety touch.

With our new pairs on, we now make to leave the inside of the shop. We leisurely place one foot and then another on the daintily carpeted floor. We glance and re-glance on the mirrored walls resplendent with dazzling electric lights of a thousand candle power that revolve and see-saw. We pass through rows upon rows of wares wrapped and coloured in all the hues of the rainbow. We notice, as we go by, the little pond and spraying fountain in the centre of the shop. The fishes in the pond swim and play as we walk away. We reciprocate the parting head-nods of the gentlemen-attendants in their neatly pressed frock-coat suits. All the while, we are slyly eyeing the beautiful lady-assistants whose last words 'Come again' keep ringing, even now, in our ears. On our way out we justle and ruffle and are justled and ruffled by the scores of bargain-hunting men, women and children. We leave all these behind. We reach the exit. The wide glass door opens of itself as we approach it, and passing through, we find ourselves again amidst the busy throng of Cheapside.

Chapter Twelve
The Word in the World

We are now at the west end of Cheapside. A huge, majestic structure suddenly arrests our attention. It stands head and shoulders
above the loftiest buildings around. Twice around its tremendous
body measures a mile. It is Saint Paul's Cathedral – the masterpiece of the architectural ingenuity of a Briton, Sir Christopher
Wren, great poet in brick and mortar.

How grand and lofty is its sky-touching dome! How marvellous
must be the geometrical staircase within the cathedral – a staircase
which, it is said, stands without any visible support. Equally wonderful is the whispering gallery which has been described, and that
rightly, as a triumph in practical accoustics. You will understand me
when I say that up that gallery, a whisper at one end can be distinctly
heard at the other, two hundred feet away; and there, the jamb of a
door sounds with a thundering roar or like an artillery discharge. It
is a place worth seeing. Let us get inside the interior of this great
and wonderful cathedral, and view there, amongst other things, the
tombs of Wellington, Nelson and Wren, within its crypt.

We now enter Saint Paul's. Its clock, connected as it is with the
great bell which, when it is quiet at night, can be heard twenty

miles away, has just struck twelve. A service, as is usual, is being held under the dome of the mighty edifice.

As we stand away from the dome, looking around, we feel struck with the majesty and venerable proportions of everything within this modern temple of Solomon. The picturesqueness of the entire surrounding makes us to exclaim within ourselves, 'This is none other but the house of God, and this is the gate of heaven.' Everything within is so grand, and yet so solemn.

If there is want of solemnity anywhere – and there is a want of it somewhere – such a sorry state of impropriety is to be seen, as you now see, not in anything attached to the cathedral, but in the regrettable behaviour of some people within. I refer to the people who do not join the worshippers under the dome. Their behaviour to us, modern West Africans, is so unexpected, that a feeling for which I cannot rightly account, moves me to versify –

> *Saint Paul's sees some just for a walk,*
> *For some there meet to laugh and talk.*
> *Some go to test the preacher's fame,*
> *Or else to meet some lovely dame.*
> *Some rush to hear the organ peal,*
> *These listen hymns, but seldom kneel.*
> *Some fancy paintings, sculpture, art,*
> *To read of men who've played their part.*
> *Some see in clothing all sublime,*
> *The great, the gay, of present time.*
> *Some pray and praise and read and hear,*
> *And these are they who worship there.*

The foregoing words – describe them as un-poetic if you like – with the following words, which you will certainly think quite prosaic if not over-prosaic, will reveal my impressions concerning the usual Sunday scenes in and out of Saint Paul's.

I remember worshipping there the first Sunday morning of my arrival in England five years ago. I saw then, therein, some people promenading arm in arm. Others merely went there to view the monuments and paintings which abound within. A few persons had sketching-books, and a number took their hand-cameras with them. The notices on the walls vainly requested that walkers-about should make no noise during divine service.

As regards the worshippers, few joined in the prayers, and fewer still answered 'Amen'. The choir for the most part sang alone. The attendance increased just before the anthem, and decreased immediately after it. The announcement of the preacher's text was an intimation for more persons to leave the cathedral. These left before sermon as if to say they were more learned than the learned doctor and preacher. I observed on that day at Saint Paul's, and on other Sundays elsewhere, that the preacher did not threaten his hearers with 'the everlasting fire and pain' as missionaries are accustomed to do in West Africa. It then occurred to me that, if really a hell-fire was wanted, Europe required it more than Africa, for on a cold winter day on this side, we could conveniently do with twenty hell-fires together.

But that is by the way. My impression that first Sunday in London was far from being favourable, especially as I noticed, on my way home, that the observance of the Sabbath was different from the mode which prevails in Christianized West Africa. I found so many shops and drinking saloons open. Newspapers were being sold everywhere. Railway and cycling excursions were frequent. Trams and other vehicles went up and down as on week-days.

I reached home to find that no one at my residence, other than myself, went to service. In fact when I returned from church, my landlady and her daughters ridiculed me for having gone. In Africa you would be regarded as a hopeless sinner if you did not go.

My landlady in trying to explain that religion was a thing of the heart and not one of forms and ceremonies, mentioned that baptism was not a condition of Church membership, that some who attended the holy communion had not been baptized, and that any stranger or visitor who went to the Lord's table would, as a rule, partake without question. She also said that she had never heard of payment by members of weekly class pence for the support of the Church. In fact, she did not believe there was such a thing as a list of Church members. She laughed me to scorn when I suggested that herself, myself, and her other lodgers should be holding family prayers. In fact I was regarded as an out-and-out heathen for having suggested a family prayer meeting. Naturally, I felt soon after my arrival in London somewhat disgusted with what I saw and heard of the religious life of the Britons. I thereupon took paper and pen and hurriedly wrote to my friends abroad, 'The Britons are barbarians and heathens.' Pardon me, I should not have given away what I wrote. Do keep my words a secret. Tell them to no Briton, for he would tear me to pieces if he knew what I had said. All the same, my words then are my words now, but the meaning has changed. I am changed myself. I have become like the Briton, 'a barbarian and heathen'.

Let me explain myself. You will remember that 'barbarian' comes from the Greek 'barbari' which means 'strangers'. Since I first wrote that the Britons were barbarians, mainly on account of my first Sunday experience at Saint Paul's, I have come to learn that the people who promenade the great cathedral on Sundays, are mostly strangers from America and the Continent. This, however, I may say in their favour – that, although they walk the cathedral, they do not in the least disturb the worshippers, for Saint Paul's is a large church capable of holding some twenty thousand people, and could therefore admit of a few hundred persons promenading at one end without disturbing the worshippers who, numbering usually two thousand, sit under the dome, at the other.

As regards the word 'heathens' which also appeared in my first letter from London to friends abroad, you will call to mind that it comes from an Anglo-Saxon word which, by extension, means 'dwellers on the *heath* or field'. The fields and heaths are the popular resorts of most Britons on Sundays. There they go to enjoy the fresh air and sunshine which long hours of labour, often in close or ill-ventilated rooms, consequent on the keen struggle for existence, deny them on other days. There some of them see God in the majesty of the sun, hear Him in the running brooks, in the gushing winds and singing birds. In this sense, the Britons are becoming heathens – dwellers on the heaths.

48

It is to be wished that the Non-Europeanized African – ancient heathen as he is, and the Briton – modern heathen though he be, will continue, in the words of Shakespeare, to find 'tongues in trees, books in the running brooks, sermons in stones, and good in everything'.

Chapter Thirteen
Sermonette After Sermon

The mid-day service at Saint Paul's being over, we begin to wend our way into Newgate Street, a continuation of Cheapside. Touching the sermon of the Reverend Doctor Doctrinabus whom we have just heard, although it is admittedly a rather learned one, yet it lacks the soul-stirring warmth of the religious discourses we are accustomed to hear from evangelical missionaries in West Africa. He deals lengthily on Predestination and Election and on the doctrine of Purgatory. To us, Churchmen, his words convey sense, but to Wesleyans or Roman Catholics, they are pure nonsense, for the Christian Church in Britain, is hopelessly divided against itself as far as doctrines are concerned. The doctors of souls like the doctors of bodies cannot agree on a good many points. Every day brings to light some 'new theology', one leader pointing us here and another showing us there, with the result that we are neither here nor there. There is quite a Babel of sects in this country. We therefore become Agnostics – 'seekers for knowledge', by sheer force of environment. We are dazed, as it seems, by the many over-dazzling and multi-coloured lights of those who would show us the way. Amidst these many lights it appears all dark. As we try to find a way through the dark, we could distinctly hear Cardinal Newman pray and say,

> *Lead kindly Light, amid the encircling gloom*
> > *Lead thou me on.*
> *The night is dark, and I am far from home,*
> > *Lead thou me on.*

Chapter Fourteen
Sects and Sets

I had said that there is quite a Babel of sects in Britain. Time would only permit me to tell you of three of them which came to my notice since my first arrival in the land of the white man. Particulars respecting the first sect were related to me one afternoon when journeying by train to the charming seaside resort of Herne Bay on the coast of Kent, in company with an old Briton of Brixton. Nice old man! He has since gone through grave to glory. He showed me when at Mid-Kent the Tower of Jezreel. This high structure belonged to the Jezreelites, a people who taught that Christ at His second coming would descend in England. So they endeavoured to build a tower the top of which might, if possible, reach up to heaven, in order that the coming Lord would first meet them in the air. Needless to say, God confused the workmen – this time not by an increase of tongues, but by a decrease of funds.

Another sect, the Pentecostal Dancers, brothers and sisters of the 'Burning Bush' and 'Pillar of Fire' mission, came not long ago to Camberwell to dance London into heaven. London, at least a part, preferred to dance the other way. As a result, the Head of the Pentecostal Dancers grew angry, and was reported to have said, 'In the whole of London there is not one religious spot, no — not one. It is a really wicked City. The task of saving it is beyond us. We came prepared to dance for its salvation just as long as we had strength and saw the slightest signs of reformation. We shall shake the dust of this modern Gomorrah off our feet. Perhaps we shall never return. It is an awful City, full of liars, babblers and people who are altogether unrighteous.'

The third sect would be most amusing but for the highly questionable conditions under which their creed is being promulgated. The members whose headquarters are at Spaxton, are known as the Agapemone, otherwise as the people of the Abode of Love. The Father Superior who is a clergyman of the Church of England, declares himself to be the Messiah.

Like the blessed Messiah, he had around him such women as Mary and Martha; and to his credit, be it said, with these he *prayed*.

Unlike the spotless Messiah, he was too fond of such women, in their original condition, as the female who, Saint Luke told us, was a sinner. He was also fond of the 'not sharp enough' sister who, Saint John said, was caught red-handed in the very act. He was also too fond of the woman of Samaria who had five husbands. The Reverend Father Superior was over-fond of Mary Magdalene with her seven devils.

On all these he *preyed*. Strong man! He *preyed* so long that there came down from heaven, in kind care of the Mother Superior and other women, birthday presents of several angels. These angels now address the Spaxton Messiah as 'Our father', in the everyday secular sense of the words.

I am not a member of the Abode of Love. Would you like to

be? I have not been to any of their *preyer*-meetings. But, I daresay, their favourite hymn consists of suitable portions from 'Where is my wandering boy to-night, the boy that I love so dear'. A little bird whispers that the service always closes with the anthem, 'Rejoice, oh young man in thy youth, and let thy heart cheer thee in the days of thy youth, and walk in the ways of thy heart and in the sight of thine eyes.'

Since the first newspaper report of the 'goings on' in the Abode of Love, the Father Superior has been unfrocked, kicked out of, and driven from the Church of England. My sympathy follows this Turkish Solomon – but may it never meet him. Let him take courage. He should remember that 'as it was in the beginning, is now, and ever shall be'. The Messiah 'came unto His own and His own received Him not'.

Chapter Fifteen
The Invisible Spirit of the Britons

I trust I have not shocked you with what I have said respecting the sect of the Abode of Love. I am sorry if I have. But if I have not, it is because good taste tells me not to go deep into details. From what you have heard, do not hastily conclude that 'the Britons are barbarians'. Remember the questionable people of the Abode of Love, the sincere but, to my mind, misdirected Jezreelites and Pentecostal Dancers, and, I may add, the Mohammedans and Brahmins and atheists and infidels in Britain, are altogether but a handful, a mere grain, when compared to the remaining Britons.[6] A rotten grain in a sack of wheat does not make the sack a rotten one. If you keep this great truth always in mind, you will not form your opinion of Britons in general from sensational newspaper reports of isolated cases of which you hear so much in West Africa.

The Britons on the whole are Christians, professed and unprofessed. Notwithstanding, I cannot conscientiously say that their Christianity is exactly that as taught by the Christ. But in essence it is. Christianity, like most other religions, is Eastern. It was originally taught by the great Eastern teacher, first adopted by Eastern people in by-gone times, and, so far, with them it worked successfully. A branch from this Eastern tree of Christianity was in time cut off, carried away, and planted in Rome. From the tree there, a branch was cut off and then planted in Britain. The soil and climate of Rome made the tree there different in appearance from the parent tree in the Holy Land, and the same cause produced the change which we notice in the tree of Britain.

I give a more concrete example. Out in West Africa, in its native home, the cocoanut tree would be higher than one hundred feet. The full-grown one I saw at the Royal Botanic Gardens at Kew, owing to the action of British soil and climate, could not be more than ten feet. The tree at Kew was in essence a cocoanut plant, for, for all intents and purposes, it would serve the Briton in the same way that the tree abroad would serve the African. The Christianity of Britain (like that of West Africa which is in turn largely a British product) is in essence that of the Holy Land, although it has been influenced by local conditions. On the other hand, and in turn, British Christianity has much influenced local conditions. It acts and re-acts on and is acted on by such conditions. It remains, notwithstanding, without question, '*the invisible spirit of the Britons*'.

There is therefore in the Briton an invisible Spirit – the God of the Word, and, as I had said a visible spirit – the god of the world. These two exist in him in a state of constant warfare. Such is the case, for 'the flesh lusteth against the Spirit, and the Spirit against the flesh'.

The invisible and the visible are co-existent in the Briton, but not co-equal. As I shall explain to you later on, the good, invisible, or Word Spirit largely influences his 'spirit of justice', and the gold, visible, or world spirit considerably dominates his 'spirit of imperialism'.

Chapter Sixteen
Mixed Matters in Mixed Company

Since leaving Saint Paul's Cathedral, we are fairly inside Newgate Street. Let us jump into this motor-omnibus, and mix ourselves with the mixed.

We get in. We are on the move. We notice that the inside and outside of the omnibus like the outside walls of the buildings by which we have passed, are covered with huge posters advertising every conceivable thing under the sun. Every tradesman and every other person is saying something about his own. Everybody is shouting. It is true that in this age of noise and bustle, only the man who shouts loudest is heard best.

Even the omnibus conductor shouts to get more passengers although we are already so many. In fact, the omnibus is crowded.

Though crowded, yet no passenger speaks to the other. But for his morning newspaper, every passenger, as the saying goes, appears quite 'alone in London'. To a countless number of Britons, and to strangers in a ten-fold degree, this Metropolis of multitudes is as lonely as, and it may be lonelier than, an African desert.

Lonely at home, lonely out of home, is this lonesome London to the ordinary lodger as distinct from the householder or any member of the latter's family. At home, it is possible for a lodger, white or black, to live a whole year without seeing, much more speaking to, any other lodger residing in the same house.

The only person whom a lodger is sure to see often is a troublesome individual in skirt and petticoat, who is known on this side as the landlady. I am not speaking of the class of landladies who try to make their lodgers feel at home when out of home. I am referring to the landlady who, always forgetting that the week consists of seven and not three days, will turn up regularly with her weekly bill every other day. One such landlady nearly caused me to be kept under lock and key, goodness knows for how long.

Imprisonment? Wait a bit; listen. After a few weeks' stay, I felt sick of her and her apartments – a feeling which comes to every lodger now and again, especially when the pudding is burnt with fire, or the soup flooded with salt water, or the basin of oatmeal crammed as if with all the fresh water of the Thames. On the occasion in question, she must have served me with one of her usual fire and water dinners, or perhaps, she was more humbugging then with her untimely bill. Her best dinner was bad. Her least bill was big.

So I decided to leave her. I made up my mind to try new rooms at a new house. In consequence, I began apartment-hunting. Whilst hunting here and there, I came across a nice-looking house at Tooting Bec Common. I at once took fancy to it. It was quite a villa – a place inside town, and yet so country-like. Groves of trees studded the surrounding grounds, and the flowers and greens leading to the porch were something delightful. I rang at the door. The porter opened.

'Well, Porter,' I said to him, 'do you keep apartments here for lodgers?'

'Yes we do,' he replied, 'but I regret we cannot receive you.'

'Why so?' I queried further. 'Do you, as a few people here, take objection to me because I am black?'

'It is nothing of the sort, sir,' he answered. 'You are not fit to stay here. I hardly think you are far gone enough to qualify you for residence. I am afraid I must repeat that we cannot receive you. To be plain, sir, this is a private lunatic asylum.'

What I *did* when the porter told me I had actually gone within the precincts of a lunatic asylum, how my heels played one after another as I jumped out of the asylum grounds, had better be left unsaid. But what I *felt* was this: I had a feeling that the best place for the landlady who nearly drove me to the madhouse, was the lunatic asylum.

However, I must not be too hard on her. Let me say a word in her favour. She has done me some service. I will say that she knows compound addition of monies better than the best Cambridge wrangler. To be exact, she knows more of arithmetic than the wrangler, since, in a clever way known only to herself, she can make three shillings plus two shillings in a lodger's bill amount to nothing less than one pound.

Excluding the fact of the necessary wrangling with her about the figures in her bill – a wrangling more wordy than the one we had in the boot shop at Cheapside – a white or black lodger, in some houses, would have no one with whom to exchange words when at home.

Out of home is worse still. The individual in a London street who seeks the company of an African, is the man who wants to know how well or how badly he can converse in English.

Another would-be street friend is the fellow who swears heaven, earth and hell that he has tasted neither bread nor water for the last forty days. If one has to judge from appearance, the fellow must indeed have been passing through an acute Lenten existence.

The other street somebody who is so anxious to make the acquaintance of an African, is the man who, thinking that the Negro stranger is a born fool, means to screw something out of him by any means, foul or fair.

On the other hand, the well-dressed chap, if I may use a collo-quialism, whose acquaintance a decent African may desire, is likely to be a person who, the next day, will send a polite note for a five-pound loan. If this latest friend does not ask for a loan, he will address a meaningless letter requesting the African to be so kind as to invite the writer and his wife to spend an evening at a theatre or a weekend at the seaside.

Even the Briton who desires to be friendly, is said to meet sometimes with this sort of humbug from the casual acquaintance. It is not to be wondered then that many persons find more desir-able friends in, and therefore have a better liking for cats and dogs.

I have touched upon a delicate question by mentioning the liking or love of some people for cats and dogs. Personally, I have no objection to pet animals. In fact I am fond of them, though my fondness has lessened since I arrived here. I daresay anyone would be less fond of animals, if he thinks how some persons, especially ladies, treat cats and dogs as if they are better than human beings.

My remarks are not concerned with the expensive purchases of cats and dogs some people make, nor with the more expensive belongings of the animals, such as sleeping cots and dinner services. I have nothing to do with the contention, as some here believe, that animals will live hereafter.

I am concerned with the excessive love some entertain for their pets, so much so, that they often forget that quadrupeds are not human. I have come across books by most intelligent men, in which the dog is described as 'him', and, at the same time, a human child is referred to as 'it'. I have seen people in Ireland, and have read of others in England who, either from poverty or affection or both, share their rooms with pigs.

I have met an otherwise decent lady in South London who would not dream of going to rest at night unless her dog reposed by her side. Her brother, for whom she kept house, frequently raised objection to her immoderate love for her pet. One day in reply to his usual objection, she seriously stated in my presence that she entertained better love for 'dear sweet puppy' than she had for her brother or any other man.

The comparison of man with dog to the disadvantage of the former being so odious, her words made me stop to think. I cannot help thinking that she has not once enjoyed a man's love. When she tries the true love of a true man, she will find it, beyond compare, more endearing than that of a dog.

I sincerely trust that she is the only woman who can give expression to this or similar utterance. When her doggish idea is getting common – and unless this excessive animal love is checked it will be common here some day – then practical moralists will be bound to suggest ways and means whereby the available aggregate quantum of national amativeness, will, with or without international or inter-racial augmentation, receive a mutual and proportionate distribution. The comparison of man with dog being so disgusting, I must leave the subject.

Chapter Seventeen
Dying and Dead

The omnibus has brought us to the end of Newgate Street, and is taking us into Holborn. On our left is the New Bailey or Central Criminal Court. On our right is the great Hospital of Saint Bartholomew which places at the disposal of the sick public about a thousand beds.

The public here do not suffer from the much maligned African malaria. I consider the malaria a maligned disease, because it has to bear, besides its own, the three-fold troubles of the three W's or woes of mankind – woes which strangers make more woeful for Africa. The three woes, as you know, are women, wine and the weed. As these three objects are so much cheaper in most parts of Africa than they are in Britain – a fact which is strange but true – they combine to produce in the immoderate stranger who has more money than he needs, or is good for him, all the symptoms of malaria.

Britons who stay at home are not so troubled. Their fashionable complaint, since the commencement of the present decade, is appendicitis.

I have been told that another disease is oblongata appendixis. My informant has not said what the latter complaint means. I suspect from the letters l-o-n-g that it has to do with the tail. I forget. Man, as evolutionists say, has lost his tail hundreds of thousands of years ago. What then is oblongata appendixis? I guess it has to do with the brain. My reason for the guess is that, as anatomists tell us, the upper part of the spinal cord as it enlarges into the brain is called the medulla oblongata.

Assuming that oblongata appendixis has to do with the spinal cord, someone has recently died of it, or of some other disease. I am led to think so by the carriage and pair of horses coming from the hospital. The carriage in question is a hearse. It contains the corpse of some victim of disease.

Perhaps if the dead man, when alive, had taken the advertised patent medicine of the All-world Cure-all Company he might not have died. That powerful elixir of life, as advertised, has been known to cure all complaints, from an ordinary fever to an attack of elephantiasis of ninety years' standing. Not having taken the 'cure-all', he died. His corpse is now enclosed in a coffin, and is being borne by yonder hearse. Poor thing!

The three men with top hats who sit on the very coffin are the two mourners and the horse driver. The driver, the man in the middle, ties round his hat a broad white band which is made to hang one or two feet behind his back. The three men are all alone, as a singing sing-song crowd of mourners do not follow a hearse here as they do in some parts of Christianized West Africa. Here, people obey the order 'Let the dead bury their dead.' As such, an ordinary funeral on this side would consist of, say, half a dozen mourners.

One of the mourners in sight is lighting a cigar. No doubt, he knows that he is not mentioned in the will of the dead man, and so he thinks fire ought to be lighted for his departed comrade wherever he may be.

At times, a fire is really lighted for the dead. The corpse is then put into a red hot oven, therein burnt to ashes which are afterwards thrown into the sea or buried. In the ordinary way, the corpse is buried in a churchyard or cemetery one or two weeks after the person is dead. Peculiar but true, they bury six or more of the common people in one grave.

Do not let the sight of this funeral mar the pleasure of your visit. 'Let the dead Past bury its dead.' We go 'on our way rejoicing'.

Chapter Eighteen
'Our Daily Bread'

Since I have been chatting, this omnibus has reached a restaurant opposite Holborn Bar, a point at the west boundary of the City of London. We now begin West Central London. It is one o'clock, the time for lunch.

We come down the omnibus, enter the restaurant, and Africanus orders lunch.

The waitress does not understand what he says, nor does he understand her, though both speak English. 'Young lady,' I intervene, 'let him start with a plate of "toad in the hole."'

Africanus, your first attempt by yourself to chat with a white lady has ended in a miserable failure. You do not understand her, because she speaks the Cockney dialect, that is, the English spoken by a common class of Londoners.

More dialects exist than that of the Cockney. There are those of Kent, Devonshire and Yorkshire, just to mention a few.

The Yorkshireman who desires to shake hands with Robert whom he meets at York unexpectedly will address him thus: 'Boob, what bring tha te Yorke this tarme o't yeer. Stop, mun, let's touch the flesh.'

Scotchmen speak an unfamiliar English which readers of Burns, their most popular poet, know well.

The Irishman I always know by his vibrating sound of the letter R. Do what you will, an Irishman will always find a Shibboleth in this sentence: 'Around the rugged rocks, the ragged rascals ran.'

In some parts of Wales not many miles away, English is practically unknown.

In the Isle of Man they speak Manx.

The restaurant waitress does not understand you, because you speak scholastic English with a West African accent. You will have to stay here several years, and pay close attention to pronunciation as uttered by refined people, before you will be able to correct the faulty accentuation introduced into West Africa by the Germans who were among the earliest missionaries and teachers sent by the Britons to evangelize the Blacks.

The best persons through whom you may better your accent are not the professors of English. As a rule, the more learned the man, the worse he speaks. Grammar will not help you much. Several grammar rules being meaningless, are calculated to arrest freedom of expression. Your best teachers of English will be intelligent ladies of the middle class. They may not know the exact force of certain words, but they do use words with a grace and a charm that are unsurpassed. For the purpose of your English, if for no other, correspond with, or meet, as many English ladies of the better class as you may, but be careful that you write or converse only about the weather and such like. If you venture to write 'sweet nothings', a single sentence of three damaging words may cost you between one hundred and three hundred pounds a word.

I trust you are enjoying your lunch. Do not expect to be served with African diet at this restaurant. The only African article of diet you may get here or at any other eating-place in Britain, is the palm-oil of Sierra Leone or of Nigeria, which after it has been made hard, coloured, and scented, is palmed off on an unsuspecting British public as best Danish or Devonshire butter. Apart from the African palm-oil-butter, there are a few fruits and nuts from our continent. And these are so dear, that the proprietors of this or any other middle-class restaurant will not think it worth their while to stock them for their dining customers. Therefore, do not ask the waitress for any food stuff that is purely African. Foofoo, our native pastry balls, you will not have. And the absence of foofoo in your dietary, you will notice on your return to West Africa, for the hot balls will then hurt, and make your throat sore.

The Briton does not eat pepper. Be prepared to put up without that. In Europe you will eat several things with which you are not accustomed. For instance, you may have to eat frogs if you go to France. The Frenchman is very fond or frogs, snails and horses. The tougher the frog the more he enjoys it. No doubt the English eat frogs as well. If not, why should they call the dish you are now swallowing with the vengeance and greed of a hungry wolf 'toad in the hole'? Has a toad got into the hole of your stomach?

Chapter Nineteen
Meditating with the Mixed

Whilst lunching in a restaurant opposite Holborn Bar, a newspaper, *The Afternoon Newsmonger*, is handed us. We observe from the headlines that it is published six times a day, and that it has half a million circulation every day. A tremendous output indeed. Yet other newspapers can boast of double or more its circulation. The proprietors are able to thrust millions of copies daily into this little world of Britain owing to the many wonderful developments in the printing machine.

I have seen a machine at the recent Franco-British Exhibition which, with two persons, can do the work of a thousand men. After it has had a feed of steam, it will take a thousand miles of paper, cut the paper into sheets, print on them, place the printed sheets together, stitch them into newspaper copies, fold the copies, pack copies into batches, stow arranged batches aside, and all that, at the rate of a hundred thousand copies an hour. One feels to admire the modern printing machine being used in newspaper work.

But I cannot admire the policy of some newspapers such as *The Afternoon Newsmonger* now in my hands. To be plain I do not care for *The Newsmonger*, because I have an idea it does not care for the Negro. It delights to report, and that often, anything wrong or exaggerated about the Blacks as would throw discredit on the race as a whole. It may be that its aim in publishing such reports is to create some sensation among the reading public, and to secure for itself larger sales in consequence. Be that as it may be, the fact remains that, intentionally or unintentionally, *The Newsmonger*, to my mind, is a mischievous organ which helps to disseminate much ill-opinion concerning the Negro.

If for a moment we overlook its Anti-Negro character, we may read it on account of the curious, melodramatic and mirth-provoking items of news which it often publishes. And so, just for the fun we may get, let us glance through the pages of to-day's *Newsmonger*. A few pages, rather columns, are the most we can find time to glance through.

Under SOCIAL COLUMN of *The Afternoon Newsmonger* is the following item: 'The Marchioness Killtime is going to spend three months with Lord and Lady Do-no-work at their beautiful castle at Idlerstown.' Although 'Satan finds some mischief still for idle hands to do', I trust His Lordship will have a fine time with Their Ladyships. He should do nothing to give more credence to the phrase, 'As drunk as a lord'.

Under the POLITICAL COLUMN a piece of news appears thus: 'In the House of Commons the member for Nervousburgh is responsible for the announcement last night that a powerful State in the planet Mars is about to wage war against Britain. The State, it is said, owns ten thousand aeroplanes to Britain's one thousand. If war is declared, it means we are done for. We shall be mere strangers in our own land.' The proprietors of this paper should know that we are all strangers here below. After all is said and done, is not the Saxon-Briton a stranger in Britain? He is a stranger here and a stranger in Africa. I wonder where his home is?

In the same column, runs something about a lady and a gentleman: 'Miss Fighting-man, the suffragette, having managed to get inside a room at the residence of a Cabinet Minister, was found tied hands and feet in his wardrobe.' Strange! Who was the first to find her there, he or his wife? If he was first, I do like to think how he would *smile*. What an agreeable surprise to him! If his wife was, I do not like to think how she would *smite*.

I now come to the GENERAL NEWS COLUMN. Something more sensational is expected: 'Burglars broke into the church of Saint Allstown, helped themselves to the communion wine and bread, emptied every farthing in the poor box, and made away with all the silver plates and cups.' Burglars are usually poor people. They took from the poor box what was intended for poor people. Therefore they took what was theirs. I see no wrong in that.

Another item of news: 'Harry Goodluck, aged ninety-nine, married yesterday at the church of Funny-side-on-sea to Jane Childton, aged sixteen.' I have never heard the like. If this old sinner was living in West Africa twenty years ago, immediately he proposed to Miss Childton, he would be mercilessly dragged by her friends into the chamber of horrors of a native surgeon, so that he could be cured of his terrible attack of appendicitis.

The following report is indeed strange: 'Jim Crow the lightning bigamist who has married, and now owns as his wives, seventy-two women living in different parts of the country, is wanted by the police.' The police had better leave the poor man severely alone. He is helping the State to solve the surplus-women problem.[7]

My spectacles are falling off, I must put them on squarely. What am I reading? 'Whilst John Manning who was convicted yesterday of house-breaking was being supplied with prison clothes in the male ward, he was found to be a member of the non-male fraternity. Manning whose second wife is still living, is said to be the father (!) of three children by a deceased wife.' The news ends abruptly. It does not state whether this 'new woman'[8] was made to occupy a male or female ward. May some kind mi(ni)ster, look after the second wife during the imprisonment of her dear husband.

Just as I make reference to a minister, I see a mention of one in this paper. I read as it runs: 'The Reverend Francis Sweeteye, a lately ordained curate, has been charged at the Bishops' Consistory Court with a serious offence against his lady-housekeeper, whereby there is "an outward and visible sign of an inward and spiritual grace".' Why on earth did the bishop interfere? Surely there is nothing wrong in the practice of some curates and other young ministers who, as a good many other bachelors do, prefer to the attendance of the landlady, the services and solace of the lady-housekeeper. The only wrong I can see, consists in the fact that the curate allowed an 'outward sign of an inward grace'. I therefore trust the bishop will not interfere with the domestic arrangement of the Reverend Francis Sweeteye and his housekeeper.

I will just glance over the next column of the newspaper.

Chapter Twenty
'In Darkest Africa'

The next column of *The Afternoon Newsmonger* is brimful with GENERAL NEWS. Time would only permit me to read a few.

The first item runs thus: 'The Society of Ladies' Tailors have decided on the extreme décolleté and sleeveless jacket, as part of the summer dress for the wearers of petticoats.' The low neck of the extreme décolleté drops a good deal below the neck of the wearer. Fancy, British ladies appearing in such a costume! But what will Aunt Grundy say? Are these ladies going to dress as do some black ones in Central Africa? To put a more general question: Are Britons becoming Africans in customs and manners? I imagine so. Africa is being imitated in more ways than one here. Already, some Britons are going bare-foot. Several have joined the 'no hat brigade'. Others frequent the heaths and fields. Others besides, sleep in the open air. Many are taking to fruits and vegetables. Thousands pass their existence below ground as do primitive men who find caves and rocks underground the most congenial places in which to live. To crown all, British and African ladies are exchanging dresses.

Listen to something, do: 'Harry Harchaic, a peasant living in the Midlands, this morning savagely assaulted an elderly woman who, he believed, had been in the habit of bewitching his family and cattle.' This reads exactly like a passage from *In Darkest Africa*.

News: 'At the High Civil Court, during the hearing of a petition for a dissolution of marriage, it was stated in evidence that the *mister* once requested the *missis* to allow some *misses* to live with them in the same house. He thought that since the more the merrier, a family of one plus seven, would be happier than a family of one plus one.' Strange! I hardly think this is a plurality of feminality; for, as we have been taught, a multiple of petticoats is known only among the Blacks. Or, is a distinguished philosopher in his book on the history of European morals right when he says, 'Chastity, in England at least, is a rudimentary female virtue, but scarcely a rudimentary virtue among men'? Perhaps, this seven plus one business means the beginning of the fulfilment of Isaiah's prophecy which predicts, 'In that day seven women shall take hold of one man.'

Goodness! what am I reading next: 'Changing husbands is a somewhat common practice in Freelifetown among a certain class of people. This surprising statement was made by a solicitor engaged in a case of which this strange practice formed a feature.' I would have considered this information as one of the usual news about the Negro, had I not read the same in my morning paper. Yes! 'Truth is strange, stranger than fiction.'

This news is worse still: 'The trial of one man who has been indicted at the High Criminal Court for highly objectionable behaviour not only towards his groom, Jack John, but also towards his mare, will come up for hearing next week.' Well!

74

Well! Well! I do not know what to say. 'I cannot speak: this fills my mouth,' as the native of the Gambia Colony would put it.

Have you ever heard the like? hale chap. The paper says, 'Professor Geologibus made a find in his garden by which he proved that people in Britain were fond of the flesh of a two-leg mammalia.' Shocking! A few months ago, I read in an evening paper that the Vicar of Braintree in Essex came to the same conclusion after making a similar find. This is like the old story of the missionary in Cannibaldom who found himself reading his Bible inside the stomach of a converted heathen. The story runs that the abdominal occupant was reading the verse which runs, 'If thy enemy hunger, feed him.'

Chapter Twenty-one
News and 'N——'

The third column of *The Afternoon Newsmonger* contains the following: 'Through Rumour Telegraphic Agency we have been informed that His Majesty's gunboat *Killman* which left here three days ago has reached Lagos, West Africa. The n—— seeing the warship fled to the bush leaving their town deserted.' I had hinted before that this newspaper is a Negrophobe publication. Apart from the epithet 'n——' to which decent Negroes object, there is a serious mistake in this telegram, if not a contemptible falsehood on the part of *The Newsmonger*. In the first place it would be impossible for the warship to reach Lagos in three days, that town being some five thousand miles away. Second, assuming it did get there then, the fifty thousand people of Lagos (a town with railway, tramway, motor-cars, electric lights, with considerable commercial and men-of-war shipping) not being such savages as this telegram would have readers believe, could certainly not have deserted their homes at the approach of a protecting war vessel. Evidently the telegram meant Lagos in Portugal. If so, how do the 'n——' come in? It is clear, to use the phrase of a well-known Parliamentarian, that there is 'terminological inexactitude' somewhere.

My eyes have just come across something more sensational: '*The Evening Scarecrow* is publishing a series of letters on Black and White discussion. The several writers have hit the n—— hard.' To you this may be bad news: to me it is simply laughable. Four years ago, another evening paper published the same kind of articles. The subject arose out of a discussion whether Negroes in Britain should be allowed to use the same restaurants with Europeans, the presence of a Negro comedian at a West End restaurant having been resented by four Euro-American diners. This was a chance for the evening newspaper to bring in two other queries by way of damaging the good name of Negroes. It asked, 'Are Negroes to be treated on terms of equality with Europeans? Are Negro students suitable friends for English women?'

In this three-fold discussion, some Americans, a few Colonials and one or two Anglo-Indians sent Anti-Negro letters. A few British friends wrote letters in defence: some Pro-Negro letters, I know for certain, the paper did not publish. Besides this limited number of Anti-Negro and Pro-Negro writers, the general public of this country by their indifference, the other newspapers by their noticeable silence, showed that evening bunkum that they were neutral in the war of the races. Britons would not be drawn into its Black and White discussion. I take off my hat to the Britons.

Before the close of the discussion, the editor tried to get me into it. He wrote to say he would be ready to publish any article from me on the subject. I did not bother to write, because I thought it was not time 'when a fool should be answered according to his folly'. If I had thought that any of his Anti-Negro contributors could be regarded as 'a fool who should be answered according to his folly', I should have answered the three questions in the following way.

The paper asked, 'Are Negroes to be treated on terms of equality with Europeans?' My reply would have been, 'The answer depends on what is the test of equality; for in some respects Negroes are superior to Europeans, and in other respects Europeans are superior to Negroes.'

The paper also asked, 'Are Negro students suitable friends for English women?' I would have answered his question by another question: 'Are Negro women in Africa suitable friends for strangers who go there?'

The newspaper's third query was, 'Should Negroes use the same restaurant with Europeans?' My answer would have been embodied in a description of the following incident which I experienced at a hotel in Bloomsbury where I was once staying as a permanent lodger. Some Euro-Americans who met me there objected to sit at table with me. The proprietor, in order to please them, asked me to alter my meal time. I told him I was not prepared to change my meal time one second to please them or the likes of their kidney. I further told the Euro-Americans concerned that as I was a permanent lodger and a British subject, I had better right to that hotel and better right in this country than any of them. That was the end of the matter. They altered their meal time which, of course, they had a perfect right to do.

Chapter Twenty-two
'N——', Negress and News

Still other mention of the Black in this *Newsmonger*. The news reads thus: 'On the ground that she is his widow by the law of her country, Miss Getsense, a Negress, has made a claim on the estate of the late Lord Mixington with whom she lived for several years on super-extra terms of friendship, until his recent death in the Antipodes. The deceased peer, a brother of the Commander-General of the British Legion, became enamoured with the Negress the first time he met her at his plantation in the Antipodes, many years ago.' I had been told that only Negroes care for this kind of miscegenation.

The *Newsmonger* continues: 'The famous traveller Dr Liarous who has just returned from a voyage to West Africa is writing a most interesting book on the customs and manners of the black n——.' What can he write after a single voyage? He is as most other writers on Negroes. They make one voyage on the waters of the coast towns at times not even landing, perhaps they take a flying trip into the interior, sometimes they join in one punitive expedition or merely spend one short term of service in a West African Colony, then return to Britain to write volumes about

Africans and Negroes the world over. Not infrequently instead of volumes, they write series of articles on the black race in some tenth-rate paper such as the one in our hands.

Do not think all papers are open to take such rubbish. There are newspapers in Great Britain which are a credit to journalism, papers edited by men of splendid intelligence begotten of extensive literary culture with a combination of wide and sympathetic views. The journalistic aims of such creditable men have evidently been to get into their papers news which are correct and at the same time proper, news beneficial to the community as a whole, news recording facts just necessary to expose vice when public policy demands it, and news applauding conspicuous acts of manliness or virtue. Such creditable journalists truthfully record the present, faithfully reveal the past and carefully indicate the possibilities and probabilities of the future.

On the other hand, the underlying principle of the proprietors of such common newspapers as *The Afternoon Newsmonger* and *The Evening Scarecrow*, seems to be, in the words of Owen Meredith,

> *News, news, news, my gossiping friends,*
> *I have wonderful news to tell.*

Their method is just to get a grain of news. This they mix up with travellers' tales or with the refuse of sailors' yarns, add to them the stuff of old wives' fables, and serve the whole concern, as a cooked nonsense, in the dish of exaggeration. Their paper thus becomes (with apology to Cowper for altering one word),

> *The fountain, at which drink the fool and wise,*
> *The ever-bubbling spring of endless lies.*

Chapter Twenty-three
Courtship Then Court

After discarding *The Afternoon Newsmonger*, a paper of questionable utility, questionable – because, it is responsible for more divorces, suicides and murders than its columns record, and after paying for our lunch, we find ourselves outside the restaurant opposite Holborn Bar.

Here on our right is Gray's Inn which with Lincoln's Inn, the Middle Temple and the Inner Temple, constitute the four existing Inns of Court. On our left nearly opposite Gray's Inn is this corner, Chancery Lane, great centre of law and lawyers. We turn down Chancery Lane. On our right is Lincoln's Inn. The Temples are at the other end of Chancery Lane across Fleet Street, the great centre of the newspaper industry.

Here, in Fleet Street, is the building of the Royal Courts of Justice. We enter the King's Bench Division of the Courts, listen to the verdict in favour of the lady plaintiff in a breach of promise case, then get out, and continue our walk, through Middle Temple Lane, with a view to reaching the Victoria Embankment.

I could see, Africanus, that you were much moved by seeing the lady plaintiff in tears. I daresay the jurors were also moved by her weeping. Her cries simply amused me, and if I had not exercised some self-control at the point where she cried loudest whilst uttering the words, 'He broke my heart,' I would have laughed loud enough for the judge to order my expulsion from the court. I had read full particulars of the case in the last edition of *The Sunday Newsmonger*.

It is the old and usual story of a handsome young man and a beautiful young woman meeting on their holiday at the seaside, the two falling suddenly in love, afterwards equally suddenly falling out of it, and then one of them – the lady usually as in the case to-day – coming before twelve jurors to secure damages for a broken heart.

This lady, as we have seen, has won the day. She has had the jurors on her side. The twelve good men and true, some of them having been convinced that she had been wronged, and some being susceptible to the charms of a beautiful woman in a more beautiful dress, were easily moved by her tears. She has been awarded damages of a thousand pounds.

Chapter Twenty-four
Black Writing Black

Indeed, jurors, as a rule, are humane. I knew this since the trial in this country of our countryman Arthur Adventurer. As a schoolmaster he had saved a little money in West Africa. He thought that his savings, besides what he might earn as a clerk in London, in addition to possible gifts from sympathetic old ladies in England, would enable him to pursue in this country the study of mining engineering, a most paying profession at his home. Had he written me before he left, I would have replied him in the following words:

My dear Adventurer,

London is not paved with gold. It is paved with stone — stone hard and cruel to those not used to paved roads. Instead of gold, we see on the roads something which for our purpose must be nameless, something left behind by the thousands of horses drawing vehicles along. If ever you get here, your first difficulty will be to prove that you understand the English language. Even the sewage-man whose English is as bad as his job, will consider himself better spoken than you, although you have graduated at a British university with high honours in English.

Still, do not expect that in this country your university degree will carry you far. Such degrees are too beaucoup *here. Every other person you meet in the street is a Bachelor or Master of Arts. Even, as a chance is, you will find that the otherwise unemployed little daughter of your possible landlady here — an under-age lass who will have to clean your boots, has graduated at a leading university with double honours in Classics and treble honours in Hebrew. It will then dawn on you that degrees are, for most practical purposes on this side, not worth the paper on which they are certified. Thoughtful people in Britain treat degrees as the builder's scaffold, things to be discarded when they have carried one (assuming that there are no shorter means of ascending) to the height or position he would reach. After one has ascended through the long-windedness of a degree and, not infrequently, even before he begins to ascend thereby, he feels the hood and the title nothing short of a nuisance. You will, I am nearly certain, feel to throw away your degree when you are in England, unless you mean to use it, as some failures here do, for the purpose of imposing on the simple and credulous. But these remarks are incidental, Adventurer.*

I had told you about the language difficulty. Apart from the people's disbelief in your knowledge of the language, you will have tremendous difficulty to get a chance to prove yourself a capable clerk. There is absolutely no chance on this side. No one, not even a Briton, can get a chance here, unless he is able to do an old work in a new way. You, being a Black, cannot get on here, unless you can start a new work of your own in a novel manner, or can do an old work three times better than the best.

Are you prepared to expend the tremendous energy which the non-recognition of our race entails on those who would succeed? If not, you had better stay where you are. Even in your own home, I know, colour puts impediment in your way. Still, I think with a little sense and tact, you will get on as a clerk or schoolmaster better there than you can in Britain.

Besides, never you reckon on the charity of British individuals here as a means of bettering your personal education or position. Remember that the Negro has been completely weaned from the suckling period of sympathy and philanthropy. He has now to creep, stand, or walk for himself and that without the help of a nurse's hand. I have to bring my letter to a close. Believe me, dear Adventurer, to be, yours truly,

A Well Wisher

Chapter Twenty-five
Black Before Britons

A letter such as the one I have just read to you, if addressed to Arthur Adventurer at the time when he decided to abandon his work in West Africa with a view to pursuing the study of mining engineering in Britain without sufficient money, might have made him stay at home. But he never received a communication of that nature, and so he left to come. He worked his passage as clerk on board ship, came, only to find here, much disappointment and sorrow. He found the raging sea of British clerkdom too cold and rough for him to swim. It was too deep for him to get a foothold. The result was, he drifted and drifted, from place to place, until his little financial strength entirely failed him. He became a financial wreck. All his money had vanished with the wind.

Thereupon, he took to open-air preaching for a living. He made himself a stump orator at Hyde Park, but was unable to get enough money by working his lungs. Things became worse, as they always have been to others in the talking profession. They reached their worst when cruel winter drove him shivering from the park.

He took refuge in a 'three shilling a week' 'fifteen storey high' room on the garret of a common lodging house in a slum district.

From his lofty retreat, he began to pour begging letters on a world which never looks up. Adventurer soon found that from his garret height it was difficult to get the world to hear him. He soon observed that the profession of begging-letter writing here, as it is elsewhere, is rather a precarious one. In Britain it is more so, for, here, it is an illegal profession. Still, he kept writing, hoping against hope.

A reply at length came. He had addressed a long epistle (an epistle as long as the longest one – that of Saint Paul to the Romans) to a rich old gentleman. In the lengthy epistle of Adventurer to Senilecus, the writer tried to prove the brotherhood of White and Black, and went so far as to promise the white-hair gentleman all the happiness of heaven if he only took pity on him as, as he said, he belonged to a distressed and down-trodden race.

The old man who evidently preferred the earthly happiness which his wealth made certain to the uncertain happiness hereafter, was too matter-of-fact for the long-winded sentiments of Adventurer. He asked his solicitor to warn the fifteenth-storey occupant that begging letters constituted the shortest cut from the height of a poor man's garret to the depth of a prison cell. The African now saw that the writing job was worse than the talking one.

What could he do next? He was ashamed to work his passage back home to meet his friends in Africa. If he returned worse than he left, it might be hellish in his own country. He had the idea people might laugh and say, 'This man began to build and was not able to finish.' He therefore decided to continue his existence in England by any possible means. I am sorry to add that he adopted means of existence which did not reflect credit on him, or on the great race which by popular sanction he represented here.

These discreditable means were gambling and betting. These however he was forced soon afterwards to give up, owing to frequent losses, and the evident hopelessness of cornering the bookie, or 'breaking the bank at Monte Carlo'. After his perforce good-bye to gambling and betting, he began to get board and lodge by false pretences. On the strength of the whiteness of the wrong side of his unwashed collar, and on the appearance of a full-buttoned old overcoat pressed to look like new, he managed to impose on credulous landladies everywhere.

To a landlady in West London he was Tom Swell, the son of a wealthy member of the Legislative Council in Sierra Leone. To another, one in North London, he represented himself as Jack Wealth, a law student. To a South London landlady, he was James Newrich, a medical student. To a fourth in the East of the Metropolis, he was Dick Merchant who had lately arrived in London with a view to purchasing goods for his trading establishment at Richtown, Diamondsburg, South Africa. He told a landlady in Central London, that he was Prince Omohoba, a possessor of gold fields in West Central Africa.

Thanks to his false representation that he is a prince! Credulous people, therefore, still believe that every Negro with a decent overcoat and a clean collar is an African prince. On the other hand, no thanks to his false representations! On account of his lies, landladies and tradesmen now make it a practice to send to an African, princely bills for beggarly supplies.

'Prince or no prince' – to use an expression of the then Lord

Chief Justice when sentencing Henry V, at a time he was Prince of Wales, for contempt of court – Adventurer met with rather unprincely treatment at the hands of the last landlady. Women are often not such fools as some men think them. The Central London landlady who was quite accustomed to the doings of flighty lodgers, British and foreign, was at least not a fool. She was sharp enough to place Prince Omohoba and his diamond mines within the iron grip of the police.

I was in court during the trial. The judge throughout the case seemed to be so much in his favour. In the words of the verdict of the jury, 'We bring Arthur Adventurer, alias Tom Swell, alias Jack Wealth, alias James Newrich, alias Dick Merchant, alias Prince Omohoba, guilty of false pretences. But we strongly recommend him to the mercy of the court as he did not know the law of the land.' One-week imprisonment was all he got. Such is British mercy.

Chapter Twenty-six
The Spirit of Justice

You see how British jurors were kind and merciful to the African. On this side, the Negro is sure to get not only mercy, but justice as well.

You remember the recent case of that soldier-lord who in his lately published autobiography wrote amongst other things of a Negro thus: 'At Cape Coast Castle we all attended divine service every Sunday. The Colonial Chaplain who ministered there was the very blackest of Negroes, but had received a university education in England. His salary was nearly £600 a year, and beyond reading the service to about thirty people on Sundays, he did nothing. I remember hearing years afterwards, but I cannot vouch for the story, that when he was dying he sent for the chief "fetish man" of the town, saying he preferred his ministrations, in which he had faith, to the consolation of the Christian religion, in which he did not believe. So much for our educated West African converts.'

When the book from which the quotation just repeated was published, the Colonial Chaplain therein mentioned had not, as a matter of fact, died. He lived to suffer by the book the calumny the good names of two other West African Negro clergymen of the Church of England suffered after they had died by the publication of a well-known book entitled *Strange Stories*. As might be expected, the much maligned chaplain brought a libel action against the soldier-lord and author who wrote that he died a believer in fetish. When the case reached the highest court in England, as it ultimately did, the Negro plaintiff was awarded substantial damages. That was British justice.

'We want justice for the Blacks and equality for the Whites, here, in South Africa.' These were the words of a distinguished British Imperial statesman who visited Cape Colony after the recent Boer War. He did not mention equality for the Blacks. Take it from me, that here, in Britain, we have already justice for the Blacks, and equality for Blacks and Whites. We shall have equality and justice elsewhere some day.

Chapter Twenty-seven
'The Law and the Prophets'

We are still in Middle Temple Lane on our way to the Victoria Embankment. You say you aspire to be a law student, just as any of these we now see, so that you may afterwards become a gentleman of the long robe. To become a law student is an easy matter. You have first of all to see the Steward of an Inn of Court. You are right to say that the word 'steward' suggests 'stew' and that 'inn' hints a place for eating and drinking. The two words have therefore indicated what you would be expected to do when a student.

Prospective law student! your work is very easy. It is all eating or drinking stew at an Inn. As a *stewdent* or student, whether you like it or not, you must eat dinners. You have to eat in the Common Room, lunch in the Reading Room, dine in the Dining Hall, during term and out of term. Huge pieces of meat and quarts of wine, you will have when dining as a law *stewdent* in the Grand Hall. As true as you will dine to-night, you will have to dine long and often, if you must be a barrister. Long – for you must dine during a period of nearly three years. Often – for you must dine every Dining Term. You will dine with great and distinguished men, such as princes, peers, statesmen, judges, admirals, generals, and may, if a member of a certain Inn, be able to say, as some of us can say, 'We have dined often with royalty.' Dinners, not study, is the primary consideration.

You will therefore do no study *unless you like*. But if you are disposed to study, read any book *that you like*, and prefer a cram coach to the Inns' class *if you like*. If you have a liking for the class, you can go to lectures on such days *as you like*. You can then attend at the middle of a lesson *if you like*. You will also sit to your examination *as you like*, in any order *that you like*, all at one sitting *if you like*, and answer questions in any manner *that you like*. Study of books, you *may* do: study of dinner menu, you *must* do. After menu study, after all the dinners, you can then be called to the Bar.

Calling to the Bar is a formal ceremony which takes place four times a year, once every Grand Night – a night with grand dinner and champagne *ad libitum*. After all have eaten well and drunk very well, some distinguished Bencher begins to make the Call. Standing in the midst of a group of equally distinguished men, he takes the student by the hand and repeats these magic words, 'By the authority and permission of the Masters of the Bench, I hereby call you to the Bar of this honourable society' – words which instantly change the student into a full-bloom barrister.

As a practising barrister he becomes a legalized and licensed liar. Pardon me, I mean a lawyer. To be exact, a student who has been called to the Bar becomes one or more of the three L's: namely, *l*iar, *l*awyer or *l*oafer.

If you prefer to be a *l*oafer, you will at last become a *l*agger, a *l*ugger or a *l*azy *l*ounger.

If a *l*iar, your duty will be to convince a greater *l*egal *l*ight who *l*ives to *l*ead or mis*l*ead *'l*even-plus-one *l*esser *l*ights, that a patent *l*arceny is but a *l*atent *l*apse of the *l*ambent *l*imb. In plain language, a barrister, if a *l*iar, has to show that *l*arceny is only kleptomania.

If after Call to the Bar, instead of *l*iving as a *l*iar you prefer the *l*ife of a *l*awyer, you will deal with *l*aches or *l*axness, *l*ivings and *l*ibels, and, last but not least, with *l*yings.

There are so many Ls about a legal light that one sometimes wonders whether *'*ell is the last living of all lawyers. George III many years ago called the volunteer corps of lawyers 'The Devil's Own'; and the devil's own they are till this day. Even lawyers sometimes say of themselves that they 'devil'; I think they devil as the printer's devil. And besides, the clergyman – the gentleman with the white gown at the top of the pulpit in the church, is even now saying of the gentleman with the black gown at the bottom of the well of the court, 'Woe unto you lawyer.' 'This is the truth, the whole truth, and nothing but the truth.'

Chapter Twenty-eight
Man and Mind in Making

We are still within the Temple grounds, and are approaching the Victoria Embankment.

On the west side of the Temple we see the Education Office of the London County Council. This office controls the public elementary training of British children in London, just as missionary societies manage the training in the elementary schools in West Africa. The public elementary schools here are divided according to locality, whereas, in West Africa, the division is based on the religious creed of the children, with the result that the leaders of religion in Britain are forever fighting with each other as to the kind of religious training to be allowed in the board or elementary schools, whilst West Africa has no such 'wars and rumours of wars'.

Irrespective of the religious training, and with regard to elementary education generally, it seems to me that the aim of the authorities in Britain, is merely to give the child a good groundwork in *r*eading, '*r*iting, and '*r*ithmetic, or the 'three R's', as these three subjects were once enumerated and explained in a speech by an illiterate alderman of the City of London. On the other hand, in addition to these subjects, the missionary societies thrust into the heads of the elementary school child in West Africa, all the knotty names in the Bible, more knotty ones in British history and geography, and the thousand and one meaningless rules in English grammar.

Poor soul! I wish his well-meant teachers had taught him more of some grammars of African languages, more of African history and geography, and less of British subjects. His teachers, notwithstanding, had an eye to his well-being. The missionaries have imparted to the West African a British education which, though defective, possesses more good points than one.

Such education admits, besides other advantages, of a possibility of comparison between the training of the British elementary scholar on the one side, and his prototype in West Africa on the other.

This comparison I could make easily, owing to several positions I held at one time or another in Britain and West Africa. As Senior Assistant Master of Saint Mary's Academy at the Gambia, I had to deal with hundreds of black boys and girls. As a Sunday worker at the Railway Orphanage at Stockwell in South London, I became intimately connected, for a long time, with nearly two hundred white boys. As manager of the African General Agency, late of Holborn, I had, during the course of nearly two years, to deal with over one hundred white lady clerks, as it was my practice to employ on mail days, at least once a week, temporary hands to assist my permanent staff.

Experiences in these different capacities teach me this: that, broadly speaking, the black child has, on leaving school, more book-learning in his head than a white one, when the already enumerated subjects, not excluding the three R's, are considered. A black child fresh from school knows, as a rule, in regard to Bible, geography and history facts, not to mention grammar rules, more than two white children put together, although he may not be as graceful in practical English composition as one white child.

Although the black youngster, when bidding farewell to the schoolmaster, may boast of more book-learning than a white one, it is to be added that, as it is often the case, the black child ceases to learn soon after school days (for he has little or no incentive to continue to learn more) whilst, usually, the white one then commences to get that practical education which alone can qualify him to graduate in the greatest, the world's university.

The British child – it is to be hoped that he duly appreciates them – has enormous possibilities for sound and practical education, possibilities far more enormous than his West African colleague has ever imagined. On this side there are, in every direction, at the disposal of the youngster, evening classes, public libraries, museums, exhibitions, botanic and zoological gardens, so much so, that the coming man in Britain would, in a year after leaving school, if he had opened his eyes, have had more practical knowledge and understanding than the West African youth who, after his elementary school days, read abroad for the University of London or Oxford. So much for their educational training.

As regards the home training of the British child, there is, as well, a difference from that of the West African. As far as I can judge, the former is taught to get for his parent love first, then respect, and the latter, respect first, then love. I have heard one

British child — and considerably more than one — address the father in such a disrespectful way as, 'John, come here.' Such words in the mouth of an African child would entail loss of all his teeth. The youngster on this side is seldom flogged with the whip. He may be flogged by being deprived of his pocket money or other necessaries. 'The rod is made for the back of fools,' is not a doctrine endorsed here. 'Beat him with the rod, he will not die,' is a doctrine which holds good in West Africa.

Chapter Twenty-nine
Africa Before Britain

We are fairly within the Victoria Embankment, an expansive thoroughfare which, in several respects, is more picturesque than any other public roadway in London. Palatial hotels, besides other imposing buildings, line the northern side. The golden-coloured Thames flowing along its southern side, combines with equally imposing buildings on the opposite side of the river, to give the viewer from the Embankment a riverscape scenery of unparalleled beauty. And to crown the delightful prospect which this expansive avenue furnishes, trees are planted on the right and left sides, after the manner of the lovely boulevards of Paris. Gardens and hangings and flowers meet the eye everywhere on the Victoria Embankment.

Amidst such pleasant surroundings is this tall obelisk monument. Fanned by the surrounding trees, cooled, as it were, by the gently flowing river, delighted, so to speak, by the gardens and palaces around, enjoying the privileges of one of the broadest thoroughfares in the first City of the British Empire, this grand obelisk is provided with a place consistent with its greatness. It is greater, in one respect, than anything Britain has, and in that respect, greater even than the Britons themselves. It lived thousands of years past, at a time when there was no Britain or the Britons as we know them now. It is the Cleopatra's Needle, a native of Africa.

Built three thousand years ago by African workmen to the order of Pharoah Necho, King of Egypt, subsequently taken to Cleopatra's City of Alexandria, this alien monument latterly found a home in this delightful neighbourhood.

It is placed here to tell the aliens who are flocking to this country, that though Britain will remain, as she always has been, the land of the stranger who cannot find a home in his own country, she only wants, and she will only encourage the best. It stands at this noble avenue here to tell us, to tell every foreigner, white or black, that a stranger of respect will, as a rule, receive amongst a liberal-minded people, any position that his ability merits. It remains here to remind Europe that Africa has a great and glorious past.

It suggests to us to look towards the Processional Way in front of Buckingham Palace. In thought, we look there. We see, as they are in reality, that the two pillars immediately fronting the palace windows are marked with the words 'West Africa' and 'South Africa' – these words and no more. We learn from the pillars at the Processional Way, we learn from the Cleopatra's monument, that in words, in deeds, the great and good will, by their interventions and intercessions with a view to lessening or nullifying the wrongs and impositions on the Negro, always bring the subject of 'Africa before Britain'.

Chapter Thirty
'Toll! Toll for the Brave'

A few yards after leaving the Cleopatra's Needle, we come to the Houses of Parliament, at the south-west end of the Embankment. We cannot enter now, as Parliament, having just begun the day's work, is closed to the public until prayer and other preliminaries are over.

So we walk into Westminster Abbey nearby. We enter through the triple portico at the north transept, pass into the gorgeous 'Solomon's Porch', the glory of the Abbey. Further inside this magnificent cathedral, we are charmed with its many multi-coloured windows. We see the lofty and imposing architectural columns, the ornamental designs of which lend a grandeur to the already glorious edifice. Within, it is so quiet and serene. It seems to echo and re-echo, 'Peace, perfect peace,' here, there, and everywhere.

Everywhere, in this hall of fame and glory, are the tombs and tablets of many of the greatest and noblest kings of England, of statesmen and orators, men of letters and men of science, painters and sculptors, soldiers and sailors, heroes who have lived for Britain, heroes who have died for her.

There, is the Poets' Corner, with the tomb of Chaucer, 'well

of English undefiled', with the busts of Shakespeare and others
who have spoken in music of verse.

Here, is 'Little Poets' Corner', at which is a window in memory
of William Cowper, who put to poetic music the celebrated judgment of Lord Chief Justice Mansfield, when either said:

> *Slaves cannot breathe in England; if their lungs*
> *Imbibe our air, that moment they are free,*
> *They touch our country and their shackles fall . . .*

That Judge, William Murray, Earl of Mansfield, who, as Bishop
Newton calls him, is 'the oracle of law, the standard of eloquence,
the pattern of all virtue, both in public and private life', has a
statue here. His memorable judgment of 1772, in connection with
the case of James Somerset, a Negro slave whose Anglo-West
Indian master would force him out of England – a judgment
which, though specially applicable to Britain, remains the Magna
Charta of Negro liberty.

We also see in this Abbey a monument to Granville Sharpe
who, because he took the case of Somerset to the Court, might be
said to be a leading pioneer in the anti-slavery campaign.

There is a monument, as well, to Charles James Fox, 'man of
the people', the great orator who exposed Warren Hastings and
his doings in India. His forensic eloquence, combined with the
matchless energy of Wilberforce and the tireless spirit of Buxton,
first made the strongest impression on Parliament and the nation
in favour of anti-slavery. He is represented dying in the arms of
Liberty, attended by Peace; a Negro kneeling at his feet is

thanking him for his efforts to effect the abolition of the African Slave Trade.

The commencement of that trade, so far as Britain was concerned, was with the expedition to West Africa, during the last reign of the Tudors, of Sir John Hawkins the adventurer. The Sir John Hawkins whose grave is within the cloisters of Westminster Abbey, is not the same as the slave dealer. The one buried here belongs to a later day. He was a lawyer and musician.

Had he been the pirate of Negroes, that great man, the anti-slavery arch-champion, would not care to be buried in this Abbey. I mean William Wilberforce. All honour to him! He effected the passing of the Act of 1807 by which no Britisher was to buy the Negro any longer. 'He was carried to his grave by the Peers and Commons of England, with the Lord Chancellor and Speaker at their head.' In addition to his grave, there he himself is – a statue, sitting.

There is also the statue of his able Parliamentary lieutenant and successor in the anti-slavery campaign, Sir Thomas Fowel Buxton, through whose efforts and those of the Anti-Slavery Society, was secured the great victory in the Act of 1833 by which Great Britain purchased the liberty of all slaves within the Empire.

Buxton, Wilberforce and Sharpe, are not the only members of the Anti-Slavery Society whom Westminster Abbey honours. There is a monument to Zachary Macaulay, third Governor of Sierra Leone, father of Lord Macaulay the great historian. There should be a monument to another member of that society, Thomas Clarkson, the immortal philanthropist, whose able essay in 1785, written in Latin in competition with other graduates at the

University of Cambridge, made Wilberforce the more determined against the enslavement of Negroes. There is, however, a
painting of Thomas Clarkson in the National Portrait Gallery, in
which he is seen addressing the Anti-Slavery Convention of 1840.

In honour of these great and good men, the abolitionists and
members of the Anti-Slavery Society, on the occasion of the centenary of the abolition of the slave trade, two years ago, it was my
privilege to convene a meeting in this historic cathedral. Over
three hundred persons kindly attended. In their presence myself
and twelve others, Africans and Afro-Americans, placed wreaths
bearing the simple inscription 'From grateful Africans', on the
tombs, statues or tablets of the abolitionists.

We had secured the interest of the Very Reverend the Dean of
the Abbey. The kind Dean first conveyed us and the large company of sympathizers over the grave of Livingstone, another
immortal resting here, who helped hardest and earliest to make
Britons better understand the Blacks. Thence, he led us to the
desired monuments. The Reverend gentleman spoke words of
love when over the statue and the tomb of Wilberforce, and con-
cluding with the beautiful language of Harriet Beecher Stowe,
famous writer of *Uncle Tom's Cabin*, he repeated, 'Remember
what God hath done: remember that this great curse of slavery
hath gone for ever.'

In our own little way, we tried, on that occasion, to do honour
to the memory of those able men who had done so much for
Africa and the Africans. Having tried our little, we left them that
day, 'alone in their glory'. We then passed out of the historic cathedral. We now pass out of the Abbey.

Chapter Thirty-one
'Wars and Rumours of Wars'

From Westminister Abbey, we pass to enter the Houses of Parliament. Fronting us in a striking manner is the lofty clock tower of this meeting place of imperial legislators. On enquiry, we are told that the dial plates of the clock are, each, twenty-one feet in diameter. It is also said that no less than five hours are taken to wind this mighty time-piece, and that Big Ben, the great bell which bangs the hour of the day, is nine inches thick. As we step within the Commons side of the House, Big Ben booms 'three' with a deep bass tone.

We are now in the Strangers' Gallery within the House.

The Commons have just begun work, the principal subject of the afternoon being the limitation of armaments. Some members are disposed to curtail the already heavy expenditure – an expenditure which tends to increase more and more, year by year. Other members are opposed to any such curtailment on the principle that he 'who would have peace should prepare for war'.

If I am to express myself on a matter which does not directly concern me, I may say, it is indeed regrettable that by this age of the world some ultimate means, other than war, has not been found for righting international wrongs. But it appears to me that before long some better determinative means will prevail. Two forces, besides a steadily growing anti-militant public opinion, tend towards this desirable end. The financial burden necessitated by the up-keep of soldiers and sailors, ships and guns, besides other arms and ammunition, will, in time, become so unbearable that some international arrangement for the curtailment or abandonment of armament is likely to result. And this wished-for result will be accelerated by the possibility that science and art will some day render infernal machines of war so destructive, that their destructive ability will, itself, destroy war; because, either fighters will not go to war since 'they will surely die', or will go to war just to die. Then, He will 'scatter the people that delight in war'. Then, 'he that takes the sword, shall perish with the sword.'

Meanwhile things will continue as they are, and may even get worse. Meanwhile, men will continue to war on land and on water. Sailors will rage the sea. Soldiers will redden the fields. From the fields the combatants will ascend to fight in the heights above, just as the ancient dwellers on the heath or field aloft themselves therefrom to live in storeys of buildings. But the storey-dwellers, tired with the heights, are, as I told you sometime this morning, now descending back to the primitive ground on the heath. In the same way, when fighters in the air are tired with the heights, when they go too high to feel that above a certain height man cannot breathe, they will come down, come down still lower, until they alight to fight on the primitive ground of arbitration. Then wars shall cease. Then men 'shall beat their swords into ploughshares and their spears into pruning-hooks: nation shall not lift up sword against nation, neither shall they learn war any more.'

Chapter Thirty-two
The Spirit of Imperialism

The House of Commons is now considering the proposed new Constitution for Disunited West Africa. Questions are being asked the Secretary of State for the Colonies respecting certain matters affecting the natives under the Constitution in contemplation.

The first questioner is Sir Charles Goodman, on whom evidently the mantle of Wilberforce has fallen. He asks, 'How is it that notwithstanding one hundred and twenty years of British rule and civilization in parts of West Africa, the natives are not considered fit to have a representative government?'

Another Commoner, Mr James Justice, a member of the Society of Friends – who 'were the first to lay a petition on the evils of the slave trade on the table of the House of Commons', and that was in 1783 – would like to know why a male suffrage clause in favour of the natives, if not a female one as well, should not be added in the proposed Constitution.

Mr Harry Hardbone, representing an Irish constituency – remembering it was only after the Union in 1801 between Great Britain and Ireland that the first Parliamentary majority against Negro slavery was secured – is anxious to know why the natives cannot be allowed to rule themselves. The Blacks are to have 'home rule', he declares. It is time, he thinks, that England in respect of Africa, should 'hands off'. He says pointedly: 'Any imperialism which does not take cognizance of the claims and rights of the black and yellow races, is selfish racialism, yea less – it is foolish nationalism.'

Mr Carr Harding, a Labour member, sees behind the present attitude of the Government towards the natives, what he describes as 'the octopus hands of the grabbing financier squeezing the life-blood of the poor and sweated Africans'.

After his remarks, a petition is placed on the table of the House, signed by the Church Missionary Society, the Society for the Propagation of the Gospel in Foreign Parts, the Wesleyan Missionary Society and other societies which have spent millions of money to educate the natives. This petition prays that the future policy of the Colonial Governments shall differentiate between educated natives and non-educated ones. The signatories think that the present policy is hurtful to the natural pride of the educated native – one who can read and write, or who, perhaps, has received a college or university education here or abroad, or who is a member of some learned profession, since, by such faulty policy, such educated native is classed with an uncivilized one, simply because the colour of their skins is the same.

Another petition is also read, emanating from the Anti-Slavery Society, the Aborigines Protection Society, the League of Universal Brotherhood and a number of kindred institutions. In this second petition it is prayed, on the assumption that Whites and Blacks are equal, that the educated natives shall receive under the

Colonial Governments and in the Colonial Civil Service, the same advantages as the Whites in regard to position or promotion. They opine that merit alone, and not colour, shall be the consideration for Colonial appointments. It is wrong, according to a case they quote, to appoint as Supreme Judge of Sierra Nigeria, at a thousand pounds a year, Egbert Englishmann who was last among successful examinees for the English Bar, whilst Professor Neil Negroman, Master of Laws, who passed the identical Bar examination with distinction, is merely appointed Chief Clerk in the Crown Law Office of the same Colony at the low annual salary of three hundred pounds. Such and similar wrongs to the natives, the petitioners think ought to receive their death-blow by the proposed new Constitution for Disunited West Africa now under consideration of this meeting of Commons.

To this and the other petitions and to the several questions asked, the Secretary of State for the Colonies merely replies in one brief sentence, a laconigram which for clearness, I am to enlarge in the following statement. He promises to advise His Majesty's Government to send out to West Africa at an early date, at least before anything definite is done, a Commission to collect evidence respecting, and to report on the advisability or otherwise of granting representative government to the natives.

Left to the Secretary of State alone, a Minister who has been reported to be sympathetic towards the natives, matters may be righted. Apart from his own wish on the subject, he has to get the collective opinion and advice of other Ministers. The Ministers would never advise contrary to what they think is the desire of Parliament, or of the more powerful body – the electors of Great

Britain. But Parliament, as a whole, is not concerned with West Africa, nor have the general electors any desire, or even any mind, on the subject of the natives. The mind of the average elector in Britain as regards West Africa is a perfect blank. He does not even know in what part of the world West Africa is. Besides, he is too busy with his own troubles to think about those of Negroes. We should therefore not expect him to express a desire one way or the other in respect of British Africans abroad. He is not concerned. The Crown Ministers know this too well. For this and other reasons, they will therefore guide themselves not by what is the probable wish of the general electors, but by what is . . .

Africanus, I should not say more. I should not spoil your already pleasant visit by referring lengthily to the peace-disturbing subject of peace-seeking politics. For the present, let me say that I do not believe in any Commission such as the one the Secretary of State promises to send out to West Africa. Several have gone out before. With what result? We know best.

Chapter Thirty-three
Negroes and N——

We are just outside the main gate of the Houses of Parliament.

A most laughable sight! This is enough to break one's sides. Do, Africanus, behave. You are in the public street. I laugh. You laugh. He laughs. They laugh. We all laugh.

A laughable sight, it is indeed, to see two Negroes arm in arm, meeting two n—— coming arm in arm from the opposite direction. 'Who are they?' you enquire. One is the chimney-sweep who is blackened by his work, the other is the n——-minstrel who is blackened for his work.

The sweep's duty is to clear all the smoke and soot inside the chimneys of houses. He, the real n——, is a contradiction. He is always cleaning, but is never clean himself.

The n——-minstrel, the other n——, goes about with a banjo and a blackened face. He thinks, and I think some people think also, that any two-leg being with a six-inch collar, a giant neck-tie and a pair of red lips on a black face, constitute a modern Negro.

On the whole the n——-minstrel is not right in his interpretation of the Negro. I cannot tell where he gets his red lips from, nor can I say where he may get his lips made plump to look as those of a Negro. Besides, his nose has to look as rotund as ours.

If the red lips and his nose are considered, the n——-minstrel does not resemble one of us.

In regard to the colour, he does resemble us. He no longer resembles ghosts and spirits. With our colour, he looks so natural. I will be able to make him out again, if ever I meet him once more with a black face. A white face is so hard to recognize when seen a second time. I have to look at a white man several times, before I can differentiate his face from that of another white person. This white n——, the minstrel, being black, it will be a delight to see him another time.

Already, he is a delight to children and many grown-up persons, his banjo and black face being the cause. His Negro-like face without the banjo is enough for some to take to him. It is true that some Whites are fond of the Negroid face of the minstrel.[9]

It is very true that some Whites do not dislike the Negro himself. It may be true that others dislike him. But it is untrue to say that all Europeans who appear to dislike him, and that all Euro-Americans, do really dislike the Negro.

Among Euro-Americans there are millions who love the Negro. Call to mind that the bloodiest and most expensive battles that the United States have fought since the Independence, the sanguinary battles of the American Civil War, were mainly on account of the Negro. Millions of Euro-Americans fought for him then. Millions will fight for him now, if need be.

Not all white Americans dislike him. In support of this statement, let me quote the present President of the United States. In his Inaugural Address, amongst other things, he says, 'Personally, I have not the slightest race prejudice or feeling, and recognition of its existence only awakens in my heart a deeper sympathy for those who have to bear it, and I question the wisdom of a policy which is likely to increase it.'

Felicitous words of the kind, or actions expressing such words, are being uttered or attempted daily by other Euro-Americans, and by many Europeans in and out of Britain.

To prove my statement respecting the goodwill of many Europeans in Europe towards the Negro, let me take the Britons in Britain for an example. Remember that they led the way for the abolition of Negro Slavery. Think how their Imperial Government once voted twenty millions of money for the redemption of black slaves, a larger sum than has ever been spent by any other Government or people, all at once, for the advancement of philanthropy. Think of all these, and more than these, think of the past, think of the present, and you will agree with me that the Britons as a whole, that Europeans generally, do not dislike the Negro.

I know you will easily recall the recent utterance of an English bishop, at a great public meeting in this Metropolis of London – a prelate whose name it will be bad taste to reveal, who is reported to have said, 'The Negro may be my brother, but it is altogether impossible to think of him as my brother-in-law.' I do not know what His Lordship really means. But I do know that his words appear to breathe dislike for the Negro. Be that as it may be, still, I do not think that the good bishop who is also a staunch supporter of foreign missions, hates the Negro.

I do not think that other Britons who have given utterance to similar words, or expressed similar words in actions, do really hate the Negro.

Such words or actions, to my mind, are but the result of an early defective training, of a misdirected education which tends to make them, in after years, when not thinking or speaking seriously, to appear as Negro-haters. Left alone to their latter-day training, a better education resulting from age-borne experience and mature deliberations, they will always say words or do things which will show them as friends of the Negro. This latter-day education gives them a feeling of liking for the Negro, whilst the early education creates a feeling not of liking.

It is this feeling of liking mixed with a feeling not of liking, which makes the otherwise friendly Charles Lamb in his *Essays of Elia* to say of the Negro thus: 'In the Negro countenance you will often meet with strong traits of benignity. I have felt yearnings of tenderness towards some of these faces – or rather masks – that have looked out kindly upon one in casual encounters in the streets and highways. I love what Fuller beautifully calls these "images of God cut in ebony". But I should not like to associate with them, to share my meals and my good-nights with them, *because they are black*.'

What Lamb has said, other friendly Britons, owing to a conflict of feelings begotten of a conflict of an early with a later education, are now saying in words or by actions. They say, 'Negroes we like you, but we have not been trained to relish your colour.'

Chapter Thirty-four
When Blacks Meet Whites

This want of relish for the colour of the Negro or ignorance about him and his colour, is more evidenced in the words or actions of the common people of the low class suburbs in Britain, by the actions of some thoughtless people of the better class, and amongst children of every class. A story or two will make this clear.

The present Alake of Abeokuta during his recent visit here, was so much annoyed by some thoughtless students of a certain British university, that prompt action was taken by the university authorities to punish the offenders.

As regards the treatment by white children to black people, an anecdote about a Negro bishop first suggests itself to my mind. The late Bishop Crowther was once spending some time in England with a white clergyman, an evangelical missionary who had been out to West Africa. The black prelate was provided with a bed on which was a white sheet. Every morning the clergyman's little daughter would examine the sheet carefully to see whether some of the blackness of the good bishop was left on it.

This puts me in mind of a story I read not long ago in an English weekly magazine respecting a little fellow who returned home from school with his copy book covered all over with what seemed to be splashes of black ink. Asked by his father to explain the filthy condition of his book, the school boy replied that the splashes were caused by a Negro lad who, accidentally cutting his finger, used the copy book to wipe off his black blood.

The other story relates to my humble self. I was once spending a day with a respectable family at Stockwell in South London. The mother introduced me to her little daughter as a person who had come from Africa. The little child looked attentively at me for a while, and then turning to her mother, asked, 'Mama! Mama! is the African gentleman black all over his body, or only in his hands and face?' The mother replied, 'Well Mary, I have never seen his body, but I daresay it is black as well.'

Little Mary, being a child who had been properly trained, did not bother to use her tongue and spittle on my hand to see if the blackness will come off. A queer white lady did use her spittle on a great-aunt of mine who was brought to England over sixty years ago.

As I speak of my late aunt, I call to mind a tragical story connected with her stay in the white man's country. Her mistress called with her to see a lady in the Midlands, a country woman who had never seen a Negro before. She was not told beforehand that she was to expect a Negro of the she-kind. In consequence, the country lady was so frightened on seeing my aunt suddenly, that, as she opened the door to her and her mistress, with one hand to the handle, she fell down dead.

Whilst this lady had a mortal dread for my aunt, both of them now far away, another lady, an elderly one, once a resident at delightful Dulwich in South-east London, was extremely fond of me. She wanted me always to visit her because, as she said, people with black hair, and black men more so, always brought her luck. On New Year's Eve, a few years ago, she asked me to call on her at twelve o'clock midnight, so that if I were her very first visitor, she would get luck during the whole year. I called on her as she desired. Strange to say, the year was a very lucky one to her. She became entirely free from her life-long rheumatism. Entirely free – in fact, more than free, for the painful malady took her to a place where 'there shall be no more death, neither sorrow, nor crying, neither shall there be any more pain, for the former things are passed away'. She has now ceased to suffer. She is gone.

I am still here, suffering from some people's dislike of my colour, especially when I visit a low class suburb in Britain.

In the low class suburbs a black man stands the chance of being laughed at to scorn until he takes to his heels. And, in such low quarters, until the Diamond Jubilee of the late Queen Victoria which by bringing hundreds of black soldiers and others into Britain make black faces somewhat familiar, bad boys will not hesitate to shower stones or rotten eggs on any passing black man, however high he may be in his own estimation.

Pray that, even now, you never meet a troupe of children just from school. They will call you all kinds of names, sing you all sorts of songs, whilst following you about until a passing vehicle flies you out of their sight.

Pray also that you never encounter a band of factory girls just from their workshop. Some of these girls will make fun of you by throwing kisses to you when not making hisses at you, whilst others shout, 'Go wash your face, guv'nor,' or sometimes call out, 'n——! n——! n——!'

This objectionable epithet recalls a funny experience I had once. I was standing with two other Africans at a corner near Chancery Lane. A poor sickly-looking man turned up and asked alms of us. We could then and there have placed him in charge of a policeman because, as I told you, it is not lawful to beg in England. But this beggar's condition was so apparently pitiable, that we raised about sixpence among ourselves, and gave it to the poor fellow. No sooner had he gone ten yards from us than he shouted, at the same time, taking to his heels, 'N——, n——, show me your tail, your coal-black tail.'

From the incidents which I have just related, you will see that the people's notion of black men is very limited, and even the limited very vague. A good many Britons believe that all Africans and even Indians in Britain, are from the same country, that they speak the same language, and are known to one another.

Of the black man's country, at least of West Africa, their knowledge is worse still. Apart from the statement that 'Sierra Leone is the white man's grave' – a wrong statement indeed – few know anything of any other country in West Africa. Many fancy that the Colony of the Gold Coast is a part of the gold district of Australia. Even their learned men find it difficult to distinguish between Bathurst in New South Wales and Bathurst on the Gambia. The editor of a leading London newspaper could see no difference between Lagos in Southern Nigeria and Lagos in Portugal. Between Liberia in West Africa and Siberia in Russia is a distance of several thousand miles; but not a few believe that the former country is the same as the latter. Not a few believe, as the beggar thought, that inside the trousers of every Negro is a tail like that of a horse.

Chapter Thirty-five
Frocks, Frills and Flounces

After leaving the Houses of Parliament, we cross into Parliament Street which together with its continuation Whitehall and adjacent streets, form the great centre of the principal Government departments, including the Colonial Office and offices of the Crown Agents for the Colonies, the headquarters of the Army and Navy, and the official residences of such political dignitaries as the Prime Minister and the Chancellor of the Exchequer. At the end of Whitehall, we come to Trafalgar Square, view there the monument of Nelson, walk through Spring Gardens nearby, thence into The Mall or Processional Way leading to Buckingham Palace, view the residence of His Majesty, pass by Marlborough House where the Prince of Wales stays, cross Pall Mall – the heart of aristocratic clubland, and reach the middle of Piccadilly. We thus avoid the rush and crush at Piccadilly Circus – the eastern end of the famous thoroughfare.

Piccadilly! – what a word? – a name familiar to every lover of fashion, gaiety and pleasure. Running near aristocratic Mayfair, once a jovial district of fairs held in the merry-making month of May, Piccadilly still remains during the day, the centre of gay, over-dressed, over-perfumed ladies – and, it is said to be the strolling-thoroughfare of the gayest and the overgay when day is done.

Even at day, I would not advise anyone to take a lady friend to Piccadilly or such adjacent centres as Oxford and Regent Streets; and few men, I daresay, would risk escorting their wives out for a stroll through any of these thoroughfares. A woman is sure to forget herself in this neighbourhood; and the married woman, although under escort of her husband, will for once, if not before, when, at such places as Piccadilly, throw to the winds her vow 'Till death us do part'. There, to the female mind 'Every prospect pleases, and only man is vile.' There, a woman must stop at every step. Why so?

Women will stop, not on account of the pickadill, a dress much worn by youth and beauty in the early days of the Stuarts, but because at the present time the sights in the shops around are simply dazzling. Frocks, frills, flounces and furbelows, meet the eye everywhere. Diamonds and gold jewellery of every kind, the latest silk gowns from Paris, velvet and satin and drapery and millinery of every make and hue – more than these – everything and all things relating to female attire of the latest fashion and description, combine to make this neighbourhood a centre of great attraction to impressionable womankind. Unless a gentleman is superfluously rich, he ought not to take a lady *into* Piccadilly.

You ask a naughty question. Don't be naughty. You desire to know whether a gentleman should take a lady *from* Piccadilly. My reply is – Take no lady thereto: bring no woman therefrom.

Chapter Thirty-six
Tête-à-Tête Through the Trees

At the western end of Piccadilly, we come to Hyde Park. Here are we in the park. It has just struck five. Crowds, the class and the mass, are enjoying the excellent music, the beautiful sunshine and the lovely flowers. You will enjoy these things, Africanus. You will also enjoy Britons enjoying them. Use your eyes on the passing men and women, and you will see strange sights just now.

There goes that gentlewoman riding her horse astride like a man. Though riding astride is not common in this country, one or two of the great and gay sometimes indulge in it.

Yonder is the belle of fashion who wears a dress which opens on the right and left of the skirt, the openings being quite above the knee. She dons 'The Directoire' costume which hails from America. When it was first introduced there, the Vigilance Society of New York tried to stop the fashion by taking criminal proceedings against the wearers, on the ground that 'The Directoire' is an eyesore to young persons of the non-female sex. But the Chief of Police not seeing things in the same light as the society, the attempt did not succeed.

As regards other kinds of dress, I have seen more funny ones in Paris where ladies may be met wearing a sort of short trousers known, I believe, as bloomers.

In Wales, I have met women wearing straw hats one foot high, and skirts one foot short: the hats are narrowed as they get to the top, and the skirts are widened as they get to the bottom.

In Scotland, men may be seen with a skirt like women's. But the Scottish men carelessly wear their skirts above the knee, and the women carefully wear theirs below the knee.

Just glance behind you. I daresay you have never seen the like. People do not consider it anything in this part of the world where everyone minds his own business. You ask whether the policeman will not interfere. Why must he? What is wrong in them doing as you see them do? Why should not a young woman sit on the lap of her young man in the public park whilst he cuddles and hugs her to himself? Parks are places for 'spooning and kissing', as the expression goes.

There is nothing strange in kissing here. It is the common form of salutation between women of all classes. They place lips to lips whenever they meet. If distance prevents lips meeting lips, kisses are thrown one to another.

It is not the rule for a man and woman not relatives to kiss unless they are sweethearts. Some fast, funny, funkless fellow thinks, sweethearts or no sweethearts, men and women ought to kiss always. He does not see why free inter-sex kissing should only be allowed during Christmastide. When it is thus allowed, he thinks that the Yuletide labial smack would be more fresh and sweet if not confined to a position under the dead leaves, within doors, of the ceiling-hanging mistletoe. Sex-kissing, in his opinion, should be every time and everywhere, and not only as between sweethearts.

The word 'sweetheart' here simply means a lover. Hence one sometimes hears a mother asking her daughter nine years old, 'When did you see your sweetheart last, won't your sweetheart come to-day?' – and such like questions.

Not only parents, but the Church also encourages sweethearting. The present Vicar of Brixton and other clergymen in London have places where sweethearts meet for the purpose of spooning and kissing.

You can therefore understand that the sexes are much encouraged to meet each other. With what result? It gives me pleasure to say that, owing to the strong current of public opinion against immodesty, owing to the fact that a girl who goes wrong is seldom forgiven and her wrong never forgotton, owing to the fact that Britons jealously guard the honour and respect of their women-folk, the freedom and encouragement allowed the sexes seldom end, as far as I can judge, in an improper manner.

Chapter Thirty-seven
'Eyes Have Not Seen'

The shady walks in the park afford opportunities for shady and unshady couples to meet. But twin souls often come together in other ways.

One other way: The beau, after the theatre, by some sort of inexplicable mistake, treads on the toe of the belle. An apology is asked and few words exchanged, or a long conversation results. In the latter case, and sometimes in the former, future meetings and appointments are the outcome.

Another way: By some other inexplicable mistake, whilst at a dance, Joan drops her fan. Joe picks it up. Thanks are offered, few words exchanged, and so on, and so on, as before.

One more instance of meeting: Jill tells her parents that she has not been feeling well of late. The hot summer days do not seem to agree with her, she thinks. She must go away for a change. She prevails upon the family doctor to recommend a stay at the seaside. Go, friend, go and see the sick Jill by the sea. 'As strong as iron', is not the word. See her with oars in hand rowing a Jim whom she happens to meet on the pleasure pier.

If you do not see her rowing, be sure, you will see her, at some quiet country dale, rambling and jumping and skirmishing with some chance gullivant. The seaside and country see many strange meetings for two.

And still other means of meeting, are those of the matrimonial agent, and of the newspaper advertisement. On the basis of one calculation, there are in Britain no less than a dozen periodicals containing nothing but advertisements of women who want men, and of men who want women.

I can understand women advertising for men. But it is surprising to think that although women are plentiful as herrings, yet some men consider them so scarce as to advertise for them. Still, so it is. The white man or woman advertises for a wife or husband when he or she requires one, just as you will advertise for an article you desire to buy.

Sometimes an advertisement states that a man wants a woman with cash. This is often the case when the would-be partner wants to rob Peter of the matrimonial market to pay Paul of the City money market. To such, matrimony is *matri*-money.

An advertisement usually states the age, occupation and other particulars of the advertiser. It frequently records all these facts or requirements, but usually omits particulars which may be necessary to the sentimental.

For instance: The advertiser ought to state whether he is the proud possessor of a pair of squint eyes. He should record whether his extra-bright right eyeball is the creation of the marble manufacturer in a Midland county.

If that is the fact, the advertiser ought not to omit to say that he has visited the dentist thirty-two times.

An advertiser ought to mention whether he is not on friendly terms with the barber. Perhaps his scalp and skull and occiput, if only we could see them, are as shiny as a looking-glass. Or, they may be compared to the glossy, hairless, fag-end proboscis of the ourang-outang.

It may be that, after all, he is in part flesh and bone, and in part wood. His legs might have been devoured by the fish you ate not long ago at Holborn.

Little that we know, the advertiser, once a worker at a meat-crushing factory, may have accidentally got his two arms chopped off by the pounding machinery. In such a case the machine, as it cannot be easily stopped, has simply to convert the human arms into sausage for somebody's dinner to-night.

You may be that somebody. I do not wish to spoil your dinner. But, in these days, when articles of food come from the other end of the universe, we cannot be too careful of what we take into our stomachs, especially if we remember that we eat pork – not from Porko in Bolivia, butter – not from Butterworth in Lancaster, and that meat is shipped all the way from the Cannibal Island.

Everything and everybody come from a long way now-a-days. Even the matrimonial advertiser often comes from a foreign country. The advertiser, as I have said, ought to give proper particulars of himself.

Proper and definite particulars are necessary, because it is possible that the fellow who resorts to the advertisement column, is incredibly small, or as one of the men of Lilliput, who, as Dean Swift in the fable of *Gulliver's Travels* tells us, was only six inches high.

These and other possible deformities, mutilations or disfigurements should be related before a definite reply is sent the advertiser.

I quite believe that some deformities cannot be revealed. Several disfigurements are internal when not external. The internal are often stomachic, and the external rheumatic. Several mutilations, disfigurements and deformities, are decidedly subpantaloonal (?).

Chapter Thirty-eight
'The Old, Old Story'

If the newspaper advertisement column is employed as a means to effect a meeting, or in whatever other way the gaffer and gammer come together, a proposal from the man to the woman is, in time, made. Sometimes the proposal is the other way about, for a few women do propose to men. But society, as a whole, is not yet reconciled to proposals from women to men.

Society, however, gives free licence on Leap Year Day; for then, a woman may propose to any man. I daresay you will like this custom to be introduced into West Africa. A nicer custom is the one on Saint Valentine's Day when a woman can send as many love letters to as many men as she desires, and a man can do the same to as many ladies as he fancies. And this Valentine love letter writing can be done with or without a view to a proposal.

After the proposal and acceptance, a match, long or short, is at once effected. Then follows that time which people regard as the best days for love and lover.

They two, foot to foot, arm in arm, are more often seen together. Hand in hand they will clasp. They, heart to heart, draw nearer. Body to body made closer. Nothing to nothing may intervene. Two sweet lips pressed in one. Kissing and caressing and teasing all the while. All the while we are here, in Hyde Park, this young man and his maid continue their kissing and caressing and teasing. Such are the usual British ways in courtship days.

Chapter Thirty-nine
Catch and Match

A love match is regarded here as two people's private business. The British mama and papa, as it is not infrequently the case, are never told that Harry has found his future better half, or that Harriet has met her twin soul.

If however the private match refuses to catch fire, the chances are that it will be made public. If it is so made, twelve good men and true will be asked to interfere. The two had the sweet to themselves: the twelve must share the bitter.

In few cases, these twelve men will be asked to see what griefstricken Harriet has done to herself from the top of the river bridge. Harry alone will be left to tell the story of the past love between himself and poor, jilted, bygone Harriet.

If Harriet had done nothing so rash, then she and Harry, face to face, would appear before the twelve men at a place of justice, just as was the case of the lady plaintiff at the High Court this afternoon, there to race with each other to tell and make public the story and reason why their private match did not catch.

To be kind, let us think that the match of love and lover has all the warmth which will make it catch. In such a fortunate case, the two will continue to make it more or less a private business until, at the fullness of time, when the consummation is to be effected before the knot-tying registrar, or, as it is more often the case, at the hymeneal altar.

During the consummation, at either place, only one or two friends, as witnesses, will be invited. These friends, as it sometimes happens, will not include the unsuspecting parents who up till now may not have heard anything about the love affair. Of course, the proverbially wicked mother-in-law to be, will not be among the confided friends who find themselves, as witnesses, before the altar.

The ceremony being over, Harriet though newly spliced, and Harry though just a Benedict, both, in some cases, go to their respective vocation in life as if nothing had happened, each wearing the ring that never comes off. Thus, many people pass from love to marriage.

Other persons, especially those of some note or position, will try to make a show of the marriage ceremony. Being showy people, and not being, at times, as wealthy as they appear, they will tell at least the furniture dealer to enable them to get household and other articles of furniture on the three years' instalment hire-purchase system. Besides the furniture dealer, other friends will be told about the approaching nuptial day. These friends, more in number, will at the appointed time accompany them to the ceremony before the altar. After the altar, not unusually, is the marriage breakfast, plenty of for-nothing wine, fine toasts, tall talks, bundles of bumptious bombastry and, sometimes, drink-begetting buffoonery.

Chapter Forty
Moon and Honey

The breakfast being over, the pair, under shower of confetti and rice and flings of old boots, goes to some quiet country place to spend their honeymoon.

I am not sure that I can relate what they do during the honeymoon. You see, I have not taken a honeymoon trip. I have not been to one. I have not read or heard of one. No pushful, cudgel-braving journalist, so far as I can recall, has witnessed or described the honeymoon doings and undoings. No imaginative novelist, so far as I can remember, has pictured for a curious outside world, the 'goings on' during an honeymoon. I am not a bit imaginative. Even, if I am, owing to personal scruples, I will not say to you, guileless young man, what I think of the doings, undoings and 'goings on' there.

Really, I cannot think anything about the honeymoon trip of the Briton. Ah! let me remember well. I think of something. There comes at the last moment into this sluggish brain of mine a pertinent story.

A little boy once asked his grandmother why he was not allowed to follow his dearest sister and her newly married husband on their honeymoon trip. 'What will dear Sister do, when she is there, Grandma?'

The old lady replied, 'Well, my little boy, you are not big and strong enough to follow them on their honeymoon trip. Sister and her husband are going a long way, through which only bigger boys with stronger bones may proceed. The bones of a little boy, as yours are, will surely break before you get to the end. There is no railway or tramway thence, for the honeymoon villa lies in some ancient country place quite out of the way. That villa is far high on the Mountains of the Moon. It is as high as the "seventh heaven" of delight. There is no trouble there. But, by Jove! the one may give the other trouble there. Yet, it is a happy place, for there they drink only honey, and look at the moon all the while. Thus the honeymoon is spent.'

There is much truth in this story, and I therefore give you it as the description of the honeymoon trip of man and wife in Britain.

After the honeymoon, they return to settle in their newly furnished home in town. In certain cases, the house is too large for them; or, the rent, besides, is more than they can afford. They therefore let apartments to lodgers. Several lodgers they find nice and agreeable and gentlemanly if not strictly religious. One lodger is otherwise. He tries to become, at last succeeds in becoming, an interloper. Then comes estrangement between the h(o)us(e)-band and housekeeper. Twelve good men and true are again asked to interfere and hear the story.

They are told that the man at the time of the marriage was not in a position to make things for the woman 'for better for worse'. He made things 'for worse for better'. It should be 'for better' first, and 'for worse' after. But the husband reversed the order.

He placed the cart before the horse. As a result, affairs got smashed. The ring which never comes off, comes off at last.

This is one out of several ways, by which happy unions here are sometimes regrettably ended. Still, it rejoices my heart to say that whatever may be the defects, and the defects are many, of the 'one man one woman' system in vogue here – in an ideal British home, one does see the excellence and the beauty of a mode of matrimony which provides that two shall 'love, honour and keep themselves, in sickness and in health, for better for worse, for richer for poorer, so long as they both shall live'.

Chapter Forty-one
Powerful Petticoats

During our chats about women, love and marriage, you must have noticed that there exists in English law, payment in the shape of damages for the loss, after a match, of a woman's love. After the marriage, damages are also given to a husband if a scoundrel make him lose his wife.

Damages are also given to, or in respect of, women against men with whom they have no amatorial or marital relations. Let me explain by a few hypothetical examples.

If for the fun of it, a man were to grasp, in a friendly way, the hand of any lady, unknown to him, whom he happens to meet along the street, the hand-shake may cost him as much as fifty pounds. Or, if he gives her a kiss, the kiss may run him into one hundred pounds. Or, worse still, if he holds her around the narrow just where her corset has full play, the grip may mean two hundred pounds from his pocket. At this rate, it does not want much imagination to see that, any man who goes about gripping every woman he comes across; will at the end of one day have lost a fortune, if he is fortunate enough not to be arrested as a madman.

If instead of forming the fool with every woman he meets, this man takes into his head to run away with another man's unmarried daughter living under her father's protection, or by highly improper means, disturb her father in the enjoyment of her services, even if she, in either case, is eighty years old, the father can recover for the loss of such services, very heavy damages against the offending man.

If she is under eighteen, and he merely runs away with her, he stands chance of criminal prosecution, as much as if he is a thief. And in the case of such running away, he may be severely punished even when he has not touched a single hair of her head, etcetera.

If she is under sixteen, and with her explicit permission, he exercises abnormally improper interference, he will probably find himself a prisoner under penal servitude during the next ten years.

From sixteen and upwards, and even from sixteen downwards, if there has been no permission for such interference, his punishment may be penal servitude for life. Before time, the punishment for this crime was hanging, blinding, or complete annihilation of the offending medium. In the case of a certain British lady, hanging is, even at the present time, the punishment for any interference abnormally improper. If anatomists say what is true, the complete annihilation of the offending medium is, in a way, still the punishment of some evil doers.

Chapter Forty-two
White Women and Black Men

Thus, as we have seen, there is always payment or punishment in respect of women in Britain. This state of things is due to several reasons, most of which are too lengthy for me to explain. One reason only will suffice now – the reason that there has always been proprietary ownership in women. Although I do not wish to take you, if I can avoid doing so, into Jurisprudence or Ancient Law, still, let me explain what is embodied in the term 'proprietary ownership in women'.

In ancient times, when men saw the curious beings we now call women, men wondered what they were. The Hebrew man thought they came from the ribs of men. Whilst the Saxon man apparently contradicting the Hebrew, seems to say that wo(e)men were 'woe to men'. Both Saxon and Hebrew and others disagreed respecting several particulars about these strange beings. But all agreed in this particular – that women were 'pleasant to the eye and much to be desired'.

Because they were desirable, these curious creatures ought to be possessed. Because some men in those early times, as some men at the present time, wanted all the beautiful women they came across, the rich bought as many as they could, as if women were goods. And because it was cheaper to carry by force than to buy, the strong snatched from their rightful owners — for then only might was right — all the women they eyed, or, worse still, chased them wherever they were met, hunting women as if the latter were wild animals. And the chasers themselves whilst hunting women as if they were wild animals, behaved like wild animals. In few words, women, in the earliest times, were obtained by force, hunted or purchased. In fewer words, the ancient man obtained ownership in women. To him women were classed and were named together with 'his house, his ox, his ass and anything that was his'.

In Britain the idea of ownership in women held good as much as it did elsewhere. Before and even after the time of the Romans, British women were hunted like animals, bought or sold as slaves.

At length, the Church interfered. Religious knights, during the age of chivalry, considering that the Holy Virgin was a woman, went about in order to protect women against the wrongs of other men. Women, in turn, gave up themselves for services in the Church. For the purposes of Church work and for other purposes, they received the rudiments of education. As time went on, they came to receive more than the rudiments. At the present time they enjoy most of the privileges of higher education.

Higher education, that great eye-opener, has revealed to some women that, amongst other things, the State imposes on them taxation without representation. Women with higher aims and better education are therefore demanding the necessary representation.

In reply to their demands, some men assert that women are not the same as men, that they are by nature intellectually, physically, morally and socially inferior to men, and that therefore it would be injurious to the State if women had the franchise. There is still no woman suffrage.

Such, in brief, is the history and the present position of women in Britain. I see in their history and present position, in more respects than ten, a parallel with those of the Negro.

One: Women at first were regarded as mere curiosities, play-things to pass an idle hour. When Negro Africa became known, Negroes were brought to Europe by twos and threes as mere curiosities.

Two: Women were subsequently bought, stolen, hunted or sold. They became men's slaves. So were Negroes.

Three: The Church by leading public opinion effected the abolition of domestic slavery of women. In the same way, the Church and public opinion effected the abolition of Negro Slavery.

Four: Education has made some British women to see that their inter-sex position is capable of improvement. Education has made some British Negroes to know that their inter-race position is capable of much improvement.

Five: Because advanced British women clamour for equal political and social rights in a country where they own land and other property, some white men try to spoil their cause by representing that women are by nature intellectually, physically, morally and socially inferior to men. The very same malrepresentation, word for word, has been made concerning advanced British Negroes when they ask for equal political and, it may be, equal social rights in their own country. But the representation against British women and British Negroes, as well as those against other women and other Negroes, are wrong, foolish and wicked. I give reasons. I must answer their detractors.

Six: Women and Negroes are not by nature intellectually inferior. At schools, they always pass the same examinations as, and not infrequently, better examinations than white men. After school they may shine less, not because they are naturally inferior, but because they have not the opportunity, necessity, encouragement or early training, to use their brains. I declare this a fact, notwithstanding the statement of dogmatic craniologists who wrongly infer inferior mentality of Negroes or women, because, as the dogmatists allege, the weight and measurement of their brains are less than those of white men.

Seven: Women and Negroes are not by nature physically inferior. It has been said that the latter though strong for primitive life, are not equal to the exactitudes of civilized conditions. If British women are trained properly, they will become as strong as women in the interior of Africa who always go farming or hunting the very day they give birth. If British women are trained properly, they will become as strong as the Amazons of Dahomey who, without proper guns, have often defeated battalions of disciplined French soldiers with all their latest arms and ammunition – they will become, to bring home a familiar illustration, as strong as the acrobatic women we see every day in music halls in Britain.

Detractors say Negroes are not strong for civilized life. I answer: If people will not carry into Africa the vices of civilization, if they do not make our continent hotter than it is by pouring therein the filthiest rum and gin, if people will not take therein their bestial practices, they will find Negroes, when civilized, as strong as they are in primitive life. Africa has enough evils of its own. It does not want the bestialities of other people in addition.

Eight: Women and Negroes are not by nature morally inferior. The findings of psychologists about the average woman are that she is morally stronger than the average man. Psychologists say that most women for months can be quite indifferent to yearnings with which men daily torture themselves. They are usually strong enough to force a bad man in their presence to be good. They could, if they would, convert a good man into a bad one. In a sense, women are morally stronger than men.

As regards the alleged moral inferiority of Negroes, I say it is a lie. I have studied the psychological temperaments of Europeans, past and present, as revealed in the doings of characters described in general literature, as revealed in the prosaic or poetic language of the authors themselves, as interpreted by actors and actresses, as demonstrated by the heroes and heroines in divorce cases – I have carefully studied comparative statistics of Europe, America and Africa, I have seen enough in England, Scotland, Ireland, Wales, France, Spain and Portugal, I have travelled considerably more than twenty thousand miles through West, South-west and Central Africa, and I say, based on what I have read, heard and seen, in different places and at different times, I have a thousand reasons, and more than a thousand, to say and prove that Negroes are not by nature morally inferior.

Nine: Women and Negroes are not by nature socially inferior. The dictates of society make them hold to-day a subject place in the politico-economic affairs of the world. In the past, society enslaved them, society taught them wrongly that God wanted them to be subject to white men. They accepted that as gospel truth. Such being the case, most women and Negroes to-day consider their respective position as what God ordained. But the more advanced ones know that nature did not intend them to be slaves to white men. It is true they have been freed from a slavery of the body. But they are still in a worse slavery. To-day, they are subject to a slavery of the mind.

Ten: The agitative British women are therefore rightly striving for equal political and social rights in their own country. The agitative British Negroes want equal political rights, if not social rights as well, in their own country. The agitative women will effect much, at least, something, before long, if they know that money and unity are the two greatest factors of strength at the present time, if they get the sympathy not so much of Ministers of the Crown, as that of the general body of electors in Britain. As things are, the agitative Negroes will not effect much for a long time, unless Negroes have money, unless they are united, unless they are less jealous of themselves, unless they study ways and means whereby they can get beyond the Colonial Minister in order to arrest the sympathy of the general electors of this country.

Chapter Forty-three
'Girls, Girls, Girls'

It is now 7.30 in the evening. We have sat here, in Hyde Park, too long. Let us rise and be going, else we become like Nicias in the fable, a somebody who, it is said, 'sat so long that he left the seating part of the man behind him'. We rise. We move away.

Africanus, I cannot take you further west, as the centre of evening merriment, though in West London, is east of Hyde Park. I am therefore taking you, back, towards West-Central London, but by a northerly direction as against the southerly one through which we came.

Here is Marble Arch, a tremendous arch or gate of marble, which for the tenth of a million pounds adorns the north-east corner of Hyde Park. We go through the Arch, enter into Oxford Street, with a view to reaching through Regent Street, a music hall, theatre or opera in or about the eastward part of West London.

I may inform you that at an opera, great singers, some of whom can command a thousand pounds a week, unite to *sing and act* some classical musical drama.

At a theatre, gay actresses, some of whom cannot command one pound a week, unite to *act and sing* some classical non-musical drama.

'Girls, Girls, Girls'

At a music hall one is treated to a variety of musical and dramatic pieces, usually short, and of a flippant character. A night's performance frequently consists of music, singing, cake-walk but no bread-dance, sand-dance, shows of trained animals, acrobatic and aquatic performances. Once in a while the programme is made more varied by songs composed or sung by Negroes, by display of boxing by Negroes, by Japanese ju-jitsu wrestling, Chinese jugglery, Indian magic and such like.

You say you therefore prefer spending the evening at a music hall. Here, at this circus at the bottom of Regent Street, is one, the London Pavilion.

Having paid for seats, we enter the Pavilion. Everything within is so brilliant and attractive. The paintings and sculpture and hangings and flowers are so ornamental and profuse. The footlights and stage scenery are exceedingly dazzling. The audience sparkling with ornaments and jewellery, dress themselves in the latest fashion. Everything and everybody being so brilliant and attractive, one's heart seems to be striking with delight.

The clock strikes six, seven, eight. The bandmaster at the stroke of eight, strikes one, two, three. 'Together!' Together, the orchestra or stringed band of a hundred performers set sweet music rolling in the air. Life comes to us afresh, and something seems to be whispering in our ears,

> *Oh! listen to the band,*
> *Ah! don't you think it grand,*
> *Do listen, listen, listen to the band.*

Presently Sam Stageman appears. With his powerful voice he sings the well-known, and, a few years ago, very popular song of 'Girls! Girls! Girls!'. These are a few of the words:

Have you ever noticed, wherever you may go,
    There are girls, girls, girls, girls,
You're petted and nursed and you're taught all you know
    By the girls, girls, girls.

Now Eve was the first girl, and wasn't she cute,
    Adam bit the apple, now we follow suit,
For you've noticed the fellows are still fond of fruit,
    Oh, you girls, girls, girls.

Chorus – *Girls, girls, how we love to please you,*
    Girls, girls, how we love to tease you,
    Girls, girls, how we love to squeeze you,
    Spooning in the park.
    Girls, you may be plain or pretty,
    Girls, you may be dull or witty,
    But, girls, there's one thing I'm glad of
    You all look alike in the dark.

While he sings the audience giggle and wriggle. They twist and turn as only long worms do when bad boys throw salt on them. As the singer ends, they give a tremendous cheer. They clap thunderously. The gallery gods vociferate and bellow, 'Again! Once more!'

Sam Stageman then repeats his song, with emphasis on the second refrain, the gallery gods joining by shouting:

> *Now Eve was the first girl, and wasn't she cute,*
> *Adam bit the apple, now we follow suit,*
> *For you've noticed the fellows are still fond of fruit.*
> *Oh, you girls, girls, girls.*

Again and throughout, the audience twist and twist and wriggle and giggle and jiggle. The singer ends, then bows and takes his exit.

Chapter Forty-four
'Pleasant to the Eyes'

The music hall band, always booming, now heralds in a troupe of six ballet girls, the professional dancers. You feel dumbstruck. Could these be human beings? – you ask. Surely, to repeat an expression ascribed to Pope Gregory, 'These are not Angles but angels.'

At a theatre or music hall, one sees the pick and prime of England's youth and beauty. Here you see women in their most pleasing form. They add to the beauty which nature gives them, an extra beauty which only art can devise. God made the women beautiful. The dressmaker made them charming. The hairdresser made them attractive. The dealers in powders and paints and perfumes made them like cherry blossoms. The milliner made then lovely. God and the dressmaker, the hairdresser, the perfumer and the milliner, together, made them half divine.

I know you do like to be amongst these ballet girls. You do feel like singing the popular song, 'Put Me Amongst the Girls'. But I am afraid you cannot get at them. If you were sitting in a five-guinea box, and had name and money, you could send word to ask your fancy to come with a friend and take supper with you and another friend after the performance is over. You four may then part in pair. But sitting as you are, in a five-shilling seat and without name or position in this country, if you send to ask one of them to meet you after the performance, you will no doubt be treated as a madman.

All you can do now under the circumstances is to do as you see others doing. By the side of your chair is a casket with a small hole. Put a sixpence into it. Now open the cover and take out the opera glass. You can, by looking through it, draw towards yourself the girl you fancy. Look. You see she is near, yet ever so far. Look, but touch not.

I should take this opportunity to give you a short lesson on the study of English beauty. Try to look with close attention on the faces of the six ballet girls at the same time. You will see quite a blend of brilliant colours on their faces. Each girl has some ten colours. Her lips are crimson, the cheeks are of a deep pink hue, elsewhere on the face is light pink, teeth white, her . . . Do not disturb me, Africanus. Do not say her teeth are not as white as those of a black lady. It is odious to compare.

Listen. Crimson lips, such rosy cheeks of pink, a lovely pinkish face and pearly teeth, are hers. Her eyeballs are white with blue or brown or black in the centre. The colour of the eyebrows varies.

Look at the mass of hair in which rests, as if in bed, her well-chiselled face. One has black hair, the second deep brown, the third blonde, the fourth somewhat crimson, the fifth silvery and the sixth golden. Such a mixture of colours! Surely the artist must be divine. That person is right who has declared that a really beautiful English woman is the most beautiful thing God hath made.

Do not be carried away by the sight of white girls, Africanus. Do not forget the glossy ebony girls you have left behind. They are sweet and lovely too. One man in the Bible who has enjoyed both white and black girls, and who is without doubt the best authority on matters relating to the lovely creatures we call women – I mean the wise man Solomon – says, 'She is black but comely.' Think of the comeliness of black girls. In figure, how full, how plump, how buxom! It has been said, 'If you hold them spooning and kissing in or out of the park, you will feel that you hold something.' Their 'Gibson' formation, to use an expression of the 'Smart Set', is all their own. There is no artificial padding there. It is all one natural lump of bump. Had I been using the butcher's language instead of that of the 'Smart Set', I would particularize their 'Gibson' *l*ump by changing the initial letter into R. Anyway, Negro girls approach better, if not surpass, the build of the most beautifully shaped thing in the form of a woman, Venus de Milo. I therefore like black girls. And I like white girls. I like both, because it is right that I should like White and Black.

Do not ask me which I prefer, white ones or black ones. I cannot answer your question, because I have never loved, nor have I ever been loved. I can however give you the answer of an English gentleman to whom I put a similar question whilst on my recent tour in Africa. He replied: 'When I am at home in England, I love English girls better, and when in Africa, black ones better.'

Chapter Forty-five
Matters Moral, Immoral and Unmoral

Still at the Pavilion. The screen is again raised. A lady performer appears.

Do, Africanus, close your mouth. For goodness' sake, behave. Remember you are amongst decent people. If you continue thus, they will think you the savage about whom they have been reading. Do not make yourself such an idiot. You rub your eyes to make sure they do not deceive you. You want to know if you are in England. You ask, 'Does she appear in the clothes that Eve wore before the fall?' Take your opera glass again. Draw her towards you. She appears indeed to be in the costume of a baby who has this moment come into the world. But the truth is, she wears flesh-coloured tights which fit her more than a glove.

Notwithstanding many could see nothing on her, yet other people would see or say something about her. Such people take objection to this kind of exhibition. As a result, one side in Britain always favours such shows, and another disfavours them.

The other day, the country fought itself most bitterly over the matter of a building of the General Medical Council which is being erected in the Strand, a very public thoroughfare. On the outside of the building are marble effigies of men and women exposing different ailments on their bodies. These nude figures being on the outside of a public building, a section of the public thought them improper.

Before the dispute about these nude marble effigies, Britain quarrelled over the costume of a charming dancer who had danced all London into joy. Her dress, some declared, was so exceedingly gauzy that she might as well be without them. Not a few therefore objected to her, so much so that when she left delighted London for Manchester, the latter city would have none of her.

Even before she came on the scene, Britain was disputing over the dress – rather, to be exact, the nil-dress – of an artiste who subsequently personated Lady Godiva at the recent Coventry pageant. To be clear, let me premise with the story of the lady whose name lent itself to the pageant.

According to the legend, Lady Godiva, who lived many hundred years ago, in order to convince her lord that she really desired a tax on the people to be removed, rode through Coventry with only the clothes which she brought into this world. When the people knew she would so ride they kept indoors. Curious peeping Tom, a tailor, who wanted to see what he should not see, was the only one mean enough to peep out. The legend states that he was struck blind. What was so forceful as to strike him blind, the legend, unfortunately, did not say.

Not many years ago, a pageant demonstrating this traditional ride was to be held at Coventry. The question then arose whether the music hall artiste personating Lady Godiva should ride uncovered as that lady did. Britain quarrelled herself nearly to death over this question. As a compromise, the modern Godiva,

though uncovered, wore a long wig of hair which hid such portions as objectors thought should be hidden.

The point of objection of this class of people – the same people
who every summer take exception to ladies and gentlemen bathing together at seasides – is, that mixed bathing and shows of
women in pre-natal costume are sure to make young persons of
the non-female sex quite queer in the head.

In reply to their objection, mixed bathers and people who frequent music halls say there is nothing wrong in mixed bathing, or
in seeing for the sake of seeing. They hold that if it is not wrong
to see nude statues in museums, it cannot be wrong to see our
gentler friends, in living form, so plain. They argue that to make
a well-proportioned statue is a work of art. They also say that for
a woman to give her body a well-proportioned development
means as good an art. But the marble-woman is a copy of the bone
and flesh one. The original is always better than the copy. Therefore, as they conclude, instead of wasting time viewing
stone-women in museums and exhibitions, it is a hundred times
much better to inspect a well-developed and beautiful feminality
having flesh and blood.

Chapter Forty-six
'Now the Day is Over'

With the crowd of music-hall goers, we find ourselves in the street at 11.30 o'clock at night. Many take friends to the famous West End musical restaurants in the neighbourhood, most of which open till two in the morning. Some, two by two, jump into close cabs and vanish. Others, still two by two, stroll through shaded thoroughfares. Others besides, the more sober ones, go home.

Those who cannot find partners among the music-hall crowd and are not inclined to go home in peace, take a walk through this open circular place which I ought to have told you is Piccadilly Circus, and get into Piccadilly, the street we see open towards us eastwards.

It is *the* Piccadilly. You would remember that this afternoon we walked through its western half. At this time of the night, like the well-known Leicester Square and all about there and all about here, it is a centre of lounge and gossip. But we cannot now go through Piccadilly. Propriety makes it not advisable for us to keep loitering under lamp posts, speaking with the eyes, making signs with our hats and discussing sweet nothings.

Besides it is too late in the night to continue our stroll about

London. I shall therefore ask the driver of this motor-cab to take us to Euston Station in North-west London. There you will get supper. You will find at Euston the midnight train ready to convey you to Liverpool, whence you will take steamer to West Africa.

Chapter Forty-seven
Parting Pats

Your train is ready to start. I must say 'Good-bye'. I trust your impressions about the Britons have been favourable. You say they are a wonderful people.

When you think on the wonderful printing machine and the underground railway and tunnel of which I told you, when you consider the great commercial hustle as well as the mighty bustle of vehicular and pedestrian traffic and the magnificent buildings everywhere such as you have seen, when you contemplate on the enormous amount of legal knowledge displayed by the learned judge in one of the Royal Courts of Justice or the wisdom of legislators in the House of Commons, when you take a prospective view of this magnificent train and the more magnificent steamer which will convey you away, you are forced to admit that the Britons are a mighty and a wonderful people, wonderful in the arts and sciences, wonderful in engineering and architecture, wonderful in commerce, in philosophy and learning.

But in regard to their social life you think differently. You see irreverence in some of the big City churches. You observe that there is rampant poverty in the midst of superfluous plenty. You have read of bestial crimes, homicides and frequent divorces. You are told there is more than a submerged tenth of men and women. You think therefore it is not true that the Bible is the secret of England's greatness.

All what you say of their social life are true, but partly true. The Bible is, in a sense, the secret of England's greatness. When you study carefully their unwritten code of social laws, you will find that many of its principles are of a Christian character, only that a modern spirit of commercialism and a sort of imperialism are trying to hush the Christian principles. It is true that the newspapers tell you of crimes and gross immodesty. They say hundreds of thousands of women walk at night the streets of the great cities and shipping towns. It is very true, as statistics tell us, that other hundred thousands are living a life of immorality, crime and poverty. But 'what are these among so many?' What are thousands to millions? What about the millions who have not bowed the knee to Baal? What about the millions of daily acts of virtue and charity which the newspapers do not bother to report? Do not judge by newspaper reports and statistics alone. Do not wrongly argue because one Briton is bad therefore all are bad. Take about the Briton a more liberal view than that of the common newspaper and the average book.

If you take a very liberal view of men and things, you will find that after all the black man is not as black as he has been painted, and that the white man is really whiter than he looks.

THE END

Synopsis of Britons Through Negro Spectacles

The words at the headings of previous chapters being rather fanciful, and therefore not being the best guide to the subjects thereunder mentioned, the following notes are intended to guide the reader; but he is advised to read the synopsis after *the foregoing portions of the book have been read once.*

'Chapter One: Taste and Foretaste' contains an anecdote supposed to be told by the author to a friend, Africanus, both being in *West Africa* about *8 a.m.*, in which anecdote reference is made to the author's conception of a white man when he was an infant, and to the fact that Blacks are not well acquainted with Whites. In Chapter Thirty-four it is shown that Whites are not well acquainted with Blacks. To make Africanus understand the Whites and Britons, a day's visit to London is advised.

'Chapter Two: Babel in Babylon' gives GENERAL DESCRIPTION OF LONDON, and facts about the POPULATION of the Metropolis.

'Chapter Three: Capital Capitally Capital' refers to VEHICLES and their users, to the 'UPPER TENS' and OVERGROUND

LONDON and to the 'SUBMERGED TENTH' and UNDER-GROUND LONDON.

'Chapter Four: The Visible Spirit of the Britons' takes the itinerants – the author and Africanus, in thought from West Africa – to the Lord Mayor, the *Mansion House* and the great FINANCIAL INSTITUTIONS nearby, bringing the itinerants to the *Bank of England* at *9 a.m.*, and the chapter concludes, after describing THE RUSH AND CRUSH of men, horses and vehicles in front of the Bank, that gold being the motive force of this rush, is 'the visible spirit of the Britons'. The invisible spirit of the Britons is referred to in Chapter Fifteen.

'Chapter Five (Chapter Six, Chapter Seven): The Man in the Street', etc. refer to well-known STREET CHARACTERS in Britain as may be seen in the crowd before the *Bank of England*. A good deal of satire is brought to bear on the London pauper and beggar.

'Chapter Eight: The Mixed Multitude' which is a continuation of the preceding, affirms that the bad is always mixed with the good, and gives examples of the kind of bad or CRIMINAL CHARACTERS one meets in West Africa or West Europe.

'Chapter Nine: Egypt's Ten Plagues' refers to THE CLIMATE of Britain.

'(Chapter Ten) Chapter Eleven: Britons, Blacks and Bargains', etc., is a wrangling between buyer and seller at *Cheapside*. It depicts TRADE SHOP SCENES in London as an aspect of COM-MERCE. For the name Cheapside and other words read Chapter Ten.

'Chapter Twelve (Chapter Thirteen, Chapter Fourteen): The Word in the World', etc., take the itinerants to *Saint Paul's Cathedral*, and after divine service therein refers to THE RELI-GIOUS LIFE of the Britons, to DOCTRINES and sermons, also to CHRISTIAN SECTS including the people of the Abode of Love on whom much satire is poured.

'Chapter Fifteen: The Invisible Spirit of the Britons' is identified with CHRISTIANITY. The visible spirit has been compared with the invisible spirit of the Britons (Chapter Four), and in Chapter Fifteen it is promised that an opportunity will be given to show Africanus that the invisible spirit largely influences the Briton's spirit of justice (Chapter Twenty-six), and that the visible spirit dominates his spirit of imperialism (Chapter Thirty-two).

'Chapter Sixteen: Mixed Matters in Mixed Company' gives the itinerants when in a motor-omnibus proceeding from *New-gate Street* into *Holborn*, a reference to the LANDLADY AND THE LODGER, to the WOULD-BE FRIENDS OF AFRICANS, and some people's excessive FONDNESS FOR PETS.

'Chapter Seventeen: Dying and Dead' tells the itinerants when by *Saint Bartholomew Hospital*, of PATENT MEDICINES, DIS-EASES and FUNERAL SCENES in London. This is a continuation of Chapter Sixteen.

'Chapter Eighteen: 'Our Daily Bread'', still a continuation of Mixed Matters (Chapter Sixteen), speaks about LANGUAGES in Britain, and concludes, whilst the itinerants are at a *Restaurant by Holborn Bar*, *1 p.m.*, with THE FOOD OF THE WHITES.

'Chapter Nineteen (Chapter Twenty, Chapter Twenty-one, Chapter Twenty-two): Meditating with the Mixed' mentions items of news altogether strange to the West African, which appear daily in THE NEWSPAPERS, and emphasizes the fact that some British writers are fond of saying ill things respecting the Blacks. The idea of 'In Darkest Africa' and of much of the preceding chapter, is to show detractors of the Negro that no crime is peculiar to the black race – a fact some white writers should always remember.

'Chapter Twenty-three: Courtship Then Court' takes the itinerants through *Chancery Lane* into the *Royal Courts*, in one of which a BREACH OF PROMISE case is being tried. There is some connection in this chapter with that of Thirty-six which is on love and marriage.

'Chapter Twenty-four: Black Writing Black' is a letter from the author to any African who intends to take up further study in Britain without sufficient money, on the off-chance of finding a philanthropic Briton who will assist him. Such an African, when in Britain, will make a possible criminal (Chapter Twenty-five).

'(Chapter Twenty-five) Chapter Twenty-six: The Spirit of Justice', etc., evidence, in the case of an African criminal mentioned in Chapter Twenty-five, and in that of an African plaintiff mentioned in Chapter Twenty-six, that the British spirit of justice as hinted in Chapter Fifteen — The Invisible Spirit of the Britons — is influenced by THE SPIRIT OF MERCY. See also The Spirit of Imperialism (Chapter Thirty-two).

'Chapter Twenty-seven: 'The Law and the Prophets'' refers, while the itinerants are at *Middle Temple Lane*, to EDUCATION in England, in respect of the LAW. A say on the mode of studying for the Bar appears in this chapter.

'Chapter Twenty-eight: Man and Mind in Making' is a reference to the CHILD'S EDUCATIONAL OR HOME TRAINING. It compares the training of the British with the black youngster, a subject discussed in front of the *Education Office of the London County Council*.

'Chapter Twenty-nine: Africa Before Britain' mentions, while the itinerants are at the *Victoria Embankment*, the lesson of BRITISH SYMPATHETIC CONCERNMENT FOR AFRICA, a lesson which is drawn at seeing the *Cleopatra's Needle*.

'Chapter Thirty: 'Toll! Toll for the Brave'' is a panegyric on THE ABOLITIONISTS OF THE AFRICAN SLAVE TRADE, a panegyric inspired at seeing their tombs and memorials in *Westminster Abbey*. The Slave Trade is at the same time viewed historically.

'(Chapter Thirty-one) Chapter Thirty-two: The Spirit of Imperialism', etc., refer in Chapter Thirty-one to the everlasting war topic in the *House of Commons* which is reached at *3 p.m.*, and the following chapter on THE SPIRIT OF IMPERIALISM which under The Invisible Spirit of the Britons (Chapter Fifteen), is contrasted with the spirit of justice (see also Chapter Twenty-six), showing that the spirit of the so-called 'imperialism' is nothing but the spirit of nationalism and selfism. POLITICS is again mentioned in Chapter Forty-two.

'(Chapter Thirty-three) Chapter Thirty-four: When Blacks Meet Whites', etc., refer to Britain's view point of THE NEGRO QUESTION, a contrast being made with that of America, and in the latter chapter a few funny anecdotes emphasize the fact hinted in the first chapter that Whites are not well acquainted with Blacks.

'Chapter Thirty-five: Frocks, Frills and Flounces' mentions about GAIETY AND FASHION, and other SOCIAL TOPICS, when at *Piccadilly*. Chapter Twenty-three and the following ones other than Forty-two also relate to social topics.

'Chapter Thirty-six (to Chapter Forty-one): Tête-à-tête Through the Trees', etc., after describing scenes in *Hyde Park* which is reached at *5 p.m.*, refers to the ever-present subject of LOVE, THE MATRIMONIAL ADVERTISER and COURTSHIP. See also Chapter Twenty-three on breach of promise. MARRIAGE, HONEYMOON and the law relating to OFFENCES TO WOMEN are also dealt with in one or other of these chapters. The subjects are continued in Chapters Forty-three to Forty-six.

'Chapter Forty-two: White Women and Black Men' is an exposition on the POLITICAL SITUATION IN WEST AFRICA, a situation contrasted with the political position of women in Britain, and the subject is therefore a continuation of Chapter Thirty-two (The Spirit of Imperialism).

'Chapter Forty-three (to Chapter Forty-six): 'Girls! Girls! Girls!'', etc., which the itinerants discuss mostly inside the *London Pavilion*, which is reached at *8 p.m.*, refers to objects or subjects at a music hall or at the seaside which strike a modern West African as strange or enchanting, such as SUGGESTIVE BALLADS, the BALLET GIRLS, WOMEN IN TIGHTS and MIXED BATHING, also NIGHT SCENES AT PICCADILLY. The nature of these subjects which are continuous to those in Chapters Twenty-three and Thirty-five to Forty-one in respect of love, women and marriage, brings us into somewhat questionable topics. As one who has to speak on the general customs and manners of the Britons, the author is bound to refer to these subjects, interwoven as they are with every aspect of human nature. It is his bounden duty to mention them, notwithstanding their questionableness; but it is hoped that the laboured attempt to clothe his observations in the most refined, if humorous and sentimental, language will render the phraseology superior to that which usually finds acceptance at the betterclass music halls in London, and the subjects palatable, if not laughable, even to Puritans and purists.

'Chapter Forty-seven: Parting Pats' in which a 'Good-bye' is said to Africanus at *Euston Station* at *midnight*, is a RESUMÉ of the most important topics discussed by the itinerants during the day. The resumé concludes that the Britons are great in art and science, and that their social life is not as bad as some newspapers seem to say, nor are Britons or Blacks as morally bad as the average book determines. 'The black man is not as black as he has been painted, and the white man is really whiter than he looks.'

Additional Contextual Notes

Compiled with the support of Danell Jones and S. I. Martin

1. Here Merriman-Labor capsizes stereotypes to startle white readers out of their racial assumptions. Many white people at the time felt comfortable with descriptions of Black people as 'human monkeys', but how did they feel about being called descendants of the 'the filthy pig'? In this joke, the author parodies European evolutionary logic when he says that because the pig's skin is white, 'the white man is a child of the pig'. Black people are quite happy to be descendants of the monkey, he quips, because it is a much more 'man-like' creature.

2. 'Fuzzy-Wuzzy'. Poem by English author Rudyard Kipling (1865–1936) published in the *Scots Observer*, 15 March, 1890.

3. Reference to the Japanese victory during the Russo-Japanese War (1904–1905). This was the first defeat of Europeans by an Asian force in modern times.

4. Why Merriman-Labor includes the coalman and dustman in this curse is unclear, but his mock-regret fashions a most fitting punishment for the men whose occupation is based on the belittlement of Black people. The burnt cork that minstrels and blackface performers used to darken themselves for their humiliating shows becomes the source of their eternal punishment in hell.

5. 'The Yellow Peril' was a nineteenth-century expression/idea that characterized Chinese and Japanese people as an existential danger to the Western world.

6. Jezreelites: followers of James White, a former private in the British Army, who took the name Jezreel and believed himself a prophet. Tower of Jezreel: constructed in the 1880s by his followers. The tower was meant to house the elect until the Day of Judgement. Pentecostal Dancers: Christian evangelicals who emphasized demonstrative worship, including jumping and dancing. They performed in Camberwell, London, in 1905. Burning Bush and Pillar of Fire: an offshoot group from the Pentecostal Dancers. Mohammedans: followers of Islam. Brahmins: Hindu priests.

7. A growing imbalance in male/female demographics in the nineteenth century led to the idea of unmarried women as 'surplus women' and emphasized the notion that a woman's essential roles were marriage and motherhood.

8. 'New woman': a phrase in the late nineteenth and early twentieth centuries for women who sought independence and fulfillment in conflict with traditional female roles.

9. Merriman-Labor stages this daring racial inversion in front of the Houses of Parliament, the epicentre of the British Empire's legislative power. As he and Africanus walk arm-in-arm, they come face-to-face with 'two n—— coming arm in arm from the opposite direction'. He suggests, at first, that the two Africans are approaching their mirror images. The situation, he writes, is 'a most laughable sight! This is enough to break one's sides.' But the 'n——' approaching them are not Black men at all, but rather white men who only appear to be Black: a chimney sweep and a blackface minstrel. It soon becomes clear that these blackened men may crudely mirror Merriman-Labor and Africanus, but they do not reflect them. Merriman-Labor plays with the multiple meanings of the slur to turn it back on itself. The chimney sweep, he jokes – who is 'always cleaning, but is never clean himself' – is the 'real

n——', the person doomed to menial labor. And the minstrel – a clownish imitation of a Black person – is merely a 'white n——', a person undeserving of respect. Because of their debased occupations, the blackened men are nothing but demeaned shadows of authentic Black men. The mirror is broken.

Although Merriman-Labor dismisses the minstrel's physical features and doltish costume as a ridiculously unrealistic picture of 'a modern negro', he jokingly applauds his blackened colour. 'With our colour, he looks so natural,' he writes. Asserting the African perspective as the norm, he flip-flops the usual stereotype that all Black people look alike. 'I will be able to make him out again, if ever I meet him once more with a black face,' he laughs. 'A white face is so hard to recognize when seen a second time.' Through this inversion, he puts his white readers in the position of having their individuality erased with a remark. Now they are made unrecognizable because of their skin colour; their humanity obliterated into an indistinguishable mass.

BLACK BRITAIN: WRITING BACK

Selected by Booker Prize-winning author
Bernardine Evaristo, this series rediscovers
and celebrates pioneering books depicting
Black Britain that remap the nation.

MINTY ALLEY C. L. R. JAMES
The only novel from the world-renowned writer C. L. R. James,
this extraordinary, big-hearted exploration of class was the first
novel by a Black West Indian to be published in the UK.

THE FAT LADY SINGS JACQUELINE ROY
A groundbreaking novel exploring the intersection between race,
class and mental health in the UK.

BERNARD AND THE CLOTH MONKEY

JUDITH BRYAN
A shattering portrayal of family, guilt and unshakable bonds as a
family's deepest secrets explosively unravel.

THE DANCING FACE MIKE PHILLIPS
A sensational, original thriller that examines the powerful link
between identity, sacrifice and possession, and questions our com-
pulsive need to chase after ambitions that leave devastation in their
wake.

WITHOUT PREJUDICE NICOLA WILLIAMS
A gripping, propulsive courtroom thriller following barrister Lee
Mitchell as she uncovers the dark secrets of London's obscenely
rich.

INCOMPARABLE WORLD S. I. MARTIN
A visceral reimagining of 1780s London, showcasing the untold
stories of African American soldiers grappling with their post-war
freedom.

BLACK BRITAIN: WRITING BACK

MY FATHERS' DAUGHTER
HANNAH-AZIEB POOL

Selected by Booker Prize-winning author
Bernardine Evaristo, this series rediscovers
and celebrates pioneering books depicting
Black Britain that remap the nation.

*'When I stepped off the plane in Asmara, I had no idea what lay
ahead, or how those events would change me . . .'*

In her twenties, Hannah-Azieb Pool is given a letter that unravels
everything she knows about her life. She knew she was adopted
from an orphanage in Eritrea, and as her adoptive family brought
her to the UK, they believed she did not have any surviving
relatives.

When she discovers the truth in a letter from her brother – that her
birth father is alive and her Eritrean family are desperate to meet
her – she is faced with a critical choice.

Should she go?

In this intimate memoir, she takes us with her on an extraordinary
journey of self-discovery, as she travels to Eritrea to uncover her
own story. With radiant warmth, courage and wisdom,
Hannah-Azieb disentangles the charged concepts of identity, family
and home. Featuring a new introduction from Bernardine Evaristo
and an updated afterword from the author, this is a timeless,
essential read.

'What a story. So vivid, honest and moving'

Andrea Levy

BLACK BRITAIN: WRITING BACK

GROWING OUT
BARBARA BLAKE HANNAH

Selected by Booker Prize-winning author Bernardine Evaristo, this series rediscovers and celebrates pioneering books depicting Black Britain that remap the nation.

A beautiful memoir written by the first Black female TV journalist about her experience migrating from the Caribbean to the UK, and the beauty and struggle of being a woman during that period.

Travelling over from Jamaica as a teenager, Barbara's journey is remarkable. She finds her footing in TV, and blossoms. Covering incredible celebrity stories, travelling around the world and rubbing shoulders with the likes of Germaine Greer and Michael Caine, her life sparkles. But with the responsibility of being the first Black woman reporting on TV comes an enormous amount of pressure, and a flood of hateful letters and complaints from viewers that eventually costs her the job.

In the aftermath of this fallout, she goes through a period of self-discovery that allows her to carve out a new space for herself first in the UK and then back home in Jamaica – one that allows her to embrace and celebrate her Black identity, rather than feeling suffocated in her attempts to emulate whiteness and conform to the culture around her.

Growing Out provides a dazzling, revelatory depiction of race and womanhood in the 1960s from an entirely unique perspective.

'A gorgeously exuberant account'

Bernardine Evaristo

BLACK BRITAIN: WRITING BACK

A BLACK BOY AT ETON
DILLIBE ONYEAMA

**Selected by Booker Prize-winning author
Bernardine Evaristo, this series rediscovers
and celebrates pioneering books depicting
Black Britain that remap the nation.**

A powerful insider exposé on the inherent systemic racism present
at Eton in the 1960s from one of the first Black students to attend.

Dillibe Onyeama was the first Black boy to graduate from Eton
College, and only the second to join when he started in 1965.
Written at just twenty-one, this is a deeply personal, revelatory
account of the racism he endured during his time as a student at
the world-famous institution.

He tells in vivid detail of his own background as the son of a
Nigerian judge at the International Court of Justice at The Hague,
of his arrival at the school, of the curriculum, of his reception by
other boys and masters, and of his punishments.

He tells, too, of the cruel racial prejudice and his reactions to it,
and of the alienation and stereotyping he faced at such a young
age.

A Black Boy at Eton is a searing, groundbreaking book that
provides a unique insight into the reverberating impact of
colonialism on traditional British institutions, and paints an
intimate picture of a boy growing into a man in an extraordinary
environment.

BLACK BRITAIN: WRITING BACK

SEQUINS FOR A RAGGED HEM
AMRYL JOHNSON

Selected by Booker Prize-winning author Bernardine Evaristo, this series rediscovers and celebrates pioneering books depicting Black Britain that remap the nation.

A beautifully atmospheric memoir and travelogue from poet Amryl Johnson depicting her journey from the UK to Trinidad in the 1980s.

'Memories demanded that I complete this book. If what I experienced was, in fact, a haunting, I believe I have now laid these ghosts to rest in a style which I hope will satisfy even the most determined ones.'

Amryl Johnson came to England from Trinidad when she was eleven. As an adult in 1983, ready for a homecoming, she embarks on a journey through the Caribbean searching for home, searching for herself.

Landing in Trinidad as carnival begins, she instantly surrenders to the collective, pulsating rhythm of the crowd, euphoric in her total freedom. This elation is shattered when she finds the house where she was born has been destroyed. She cannot – nor wants to – escape from the inheritance of colonialism.

Her bittersweet welcome sets the tone for her intoxicating exploration of these distinct islands. In evocative, lyrical prose, *Sequins for a Ragged Hem* is an astonishingly unique memoir, interrogating the way our past and present selves live alongside each other.

He just wanted a decent book to read ...

Not too much to ask, is it? It was in 1935 when Allen Lane, Managing
Director of Bodley Head Publishers, stood on a platform at Exeter railway
station looking for something good to read on his journey back to London.
His choice was limited to popular magazines and poor-quality paperbacks –
the same choice faced every day by the vast majority of readers, few of
whom could afford hardbacks. Lane's disappointment and subsequent anger
at the range of books generally available led him to found a company – and
change the world.

*'We believed in the existence in this country of a vast reading public for intelligent
books at a low price, and staked everything on it'*
Sir Allen Lane, 1902–1970, founder of Penguin Books

The quality paperback had arrived – and not just in bookshops. Lane was
adamant that his Penguins should appear in chain stores and tobacconists,
and should cost no more than a packet of cigarettes.

Reading habits (and cigarette prices) have changed since 1935, but
Penguin still believes in publishing the best books for everybody to
enjoy. We still believe that good design costs no more than bad design,
and we still believe that quality books published passionately and responsibly
make the world a better place.

So wherever you see the little bird – whether it's on a piece of
prize-winning literary fiction or a celebrity autobiography, political tour
de force or historical masterpiece, a serial-killer thriller, reference book,
world classic or a piece of pure escapism – you can bet that it represents
the very best that the genre has to offer.

Whatever you like to read – trust Penguin.